JOANNA HOGG & ADAM ROBERTS

Chantal Akerman Retrospective Handbook

A Nos Amours

Published in London by A Nos Amours

Book design by Lora Findlay

Printed in the European Union

ISBN: 978-1-9161537-0-7

Visit A Nos Amours on the web at www.anosamours.co.uk

JOANNA HOGG & ADAM ROBERTS

Chantal Akerman Retrospective Handbook

A Nos Amours

Contents

Foreword

BY LAURA MULVEY

I WOULD LIKE to begin by thanking *A Nos Amours* (Joanna Hogg and Adam Roberts) for inviting me to write a foreword to this remarkable publication, the *Chantal Akerman Retrospective Handbook*, a memorial to an extraordinary enterprise: the only complete retrospective of Chantal Akerman's films yet held, programmed between November 2013 and October 2015, and evocatively described by *A Nos Amours* as a 'slow retrospective'. The *Handbook* necessarily looks, as it were, in two directions: towards the future and to the past, simultaneously practical and poetic. Obviously and practically, it addresses the future, giving essential, detailed documentation about Akerman's films, accompanied by useful critical perspectives and, as such, it will stand as an invaluable point of reference for Akerman curators and programmers of all kinds. Furthermore, and more generally, the *Handbook* gives fascinating, and equally invaluable, information about the difficulties and the possibilities involved in creating an exhaustive programme of this kind with minimal resources, passing on a certain kind of curatorial 'lore': the difficulty of actually finding prints, their varied states of deterioration, the tireless and unpaid work of translation, of creating subtitles and transferring them onto the print, sometimes even 'live' during the screening. But the *Handbook* also has a more emotional current running through it, leading back into the past of the retrospective itself and to the deeper, poetic implications of the enterprise. While literally memorialising the progress of the screenings, the publication of the book is the 'tip of an iceberg'. It bears witness to processes of organisation and critical engagement but also to the pure passion for Akerman's cinema that brought together the two main initiators but also, as the *Handbook* emphasises, the team of collaborators who made the programmes possible across such an extended period of time. This unusual sense of dedication runs throughout the publication, spreading out from the core organising group to the 'Akerman audience' as the retrospective gained momentum, and generated special events: the theatrical release of *je tu il elle* in March 2015, the halfway Symposium in October 2014, the 'Akerman Now' exhibition at Ambika P3 in October 2015, and finally an international conference in November 2016.

But on another emotional and poetic level, the *Handbook* is necessarily deeply rooted in the past. Chantal Akerman died on 5th October 2015 just as she herself was expected to arrive in London for the opening of her exhibition and as the retrospective was about to end. Inevitably, the publication is a memorial not only to the retrospective, but also to Akerman herself.

Given the Introduction's diary-like format she is, throughout, alive, present and vibrant as the relation between the programmers and the director grew and developed over the two-year period. Akerman, helpful and cooperative from the very beginning, became increasingly personally involved with the *A Nos Amours* programme, appearing at one of the screenings in May 2015 and then at the Symposium. But her death threw a tragic, retrospective shadow over the previous two years. As the Introduction recounts:

'In terms of the retrospective, the penultimate screening, of *La Folie Almayer*, was scheduled to take place on 22nd October. This screening was suddenly and shockingly therefore to be a posthumous screening'.

The book is inevitably a celebration of a finished body of work but it also documents the strong and dynamic presence Chantal Akerman exerted in her lifetime.

Alongside the accumulating aesthetic and emotional impact
of the films, Akerman's presence emerges and persists in
complicated ways that are specific to her personal relation to the
cinema, something that goes far beyond the usual experience
of a director, personal and aesthetic, in a retrospective. In the
first instance, Akerman's actual bodily appearances on the
screen inevitably contribute to this sense of presence, further
intensified by *A Nos Amours*'s decision to show the films in
chronological order. From her first film *Saute ma ville* (1968) to
her last, a portrait of her mother, *No Home Movie*, released in
2015, Akerman moves easily from one side of the camera to the
other, sometimes as herself, sometimes in a fictional persona.
From early on her work as a director had been documented,
for instance, in Sami Frey's *Autour de Jeanne Dielman* (1976),
but most particularly in the remarkable self-portraits made
for television in the 1980s and 90s as her reputation grew.
Her powerful and articulate personality, her charm and her
photogenic relation to the camera, the dramatic records of
her directorial processes, stand vividly alongside her fictional
appearances, so that the distinction between the Akerman
documentary portrait and the Akerman performance almost
begin to blur. The inclusion of all the relevant film material is
crucial to this sense of interaction between documentary and
fiction and the fluidity between appearance and authorship
in the short, more fragmentary, often personal, films gives
a crucial underpinning to these themes in Akerman's more
formal features. If I have often commented on the way that
cinema fuses the animate and the inanimate, giving an illusion
of movement to stillness and preserving the presence of its
ghostly figures long after their death, this thought is particularly
apposite for Akerman. Her physical presence, the traces of her
unmistakable bodily movements and her extraordinary beauty
on the screen retrospectively extend to her personal imprint
on those films in which she does not actually appear herself,

as though her passions, obsessions and preoccupations could become something like an indexical marker 'Chantal'.

To reiterate: this sense of indelible presence has come across to me very strongly through the structure of the retrospective that the *Handbook* reflects, due to the inclusion of every single Akerman film, accompanied by programme notes (with date/running time/format etc) and in chronological order. I want only to make a few observations here that have come to me directly from thinking back to the retrospective through the medium of the *Handbook*, a practical example of its uses as an aide-mémoire. For instance, looking at the rhythm and structure of Akerman's work chronologically, I realised that certain films stand as specific high points that collect other films into patterns of theme and preoccupation around them.

Obviously, *Jeanne Dielman*, *23 Quai du Commerce, 1080 Bruxelles* in 1976 creates a central point for Akerman's 1970s, bringing the formal ideas of her early New York films into a dynamic encounter with feminism's focus on stories and images of women. *Jeanne Dielman* is bracketed by two intensely personal films, in the first of which, *je tu il elle*, Akerman is constantly, chaotically and uncompromisingly on screen, and in the second, *News from home*, she is only present on the soundtrack accompanying the exquisitely composed, mostly static, highly photographic shots of New York. These films belong to the 1970s wave of women's filmmaking and had such a crucial influence on so many of us at the time and led logically to the 1978 story of a successful young woman filmmaker's nomadic journey from screening to screening in *Les Rendez-vous d'Anna*. Akerman's extraordinary contribution to the 1970s feminist challenge to cinema as such is inextricably bound up in that political moment and its encounter with a radical film aesthetic. Both the overarching consciousness of a women's movement and the framework of film formalism fell into decline with the very different constraints of the following decade. Although, to my mind, Akerman contributed crucially to women's cinema throughout the rest of her career, her 70s films have a particular relationship to that moment of excitement and discovery.

Akerman's early 1980s revolve around *Golden Eighties*, a big-budget musical, set in a shopping mall, that she finally produced in 1986. But during the development process, she experimented with the formal implications of this shift towards melodrama, music and emotion. In the extraordinary *Toute une nuit*, made in 1982, Akerman's rehearses her themes of amour fou, erotic indecision, loneliness and abandonment in tableaux of song, dance and highly gestural performance to create a completely new and minimalist form of melodrama. Adam Roberts has pointed out that, in spite of its glossy look and commercial aspirations, *Golden Eighties* reflects the economic hardship of the times, in keeping, perhaps, with the flowering of Hollywood musicals during the Depression of the 1930s. The film was not a critical or commercial success. From an aesthetic and narrative perspective, however, *Golden Eighties* is a significant development for Akerman, taking her play with seriality, for instance, beyond the sequential structure of shots and scenes into the form, even the materiality, of the film. The chorus line, with its series of similar but slightly differentiated figures, generates its own repetitive pattern through repeated motifs of song and dance, and gossip passes in a chain formation from young woman to young woman, framed by the mirrors of a hairdresser's salon. The film demonstrates the way that linear patterns can postpone, rather than lead to, conclusion.

While she was developing *Golden Eighties*, Akerman made some remarkable short films, commissions from the newly established, more 'experimental' television stations that appeared around this time. My favourite is *Portrait d'une paresseuse* in which Akerman's own performance of slothfulness envelops the film itself. The spectator gradually realises that the procrastinating director on screen ('To make a film one must get up!' – an echo of *Lettre de cinéaste*) is too lazy to shoot more footage for her film: *Portrait d'une paresseuse* begins, continues a bit and then returns to the beginning and repeats its earlier scenes until it runs out of energy altogether. But this witty device also draws attention to series and repetition as postponement, a refusal of forward movement and an intense interest in exploring ways of holding time in check, spatialising temporality, as it were. Once again, pattern and repetition as resistance to narrative also are a reminder of Akerman's involvement with the patterns and repetitions of music, specifically found in her friendship with the cellist, Sonia Wieder-Atherton, and the short music films of the late 1990s. But, and a big but, and needless to say: any analysis of Akerman has to face unpredictability and divergence from any straightforward decade-by-decade system. In 1983, *L'Homme à la valise* picks up from *Les Rendez-vous d'Anna* as Chantal returns from a film tour to find an unwelcome guest in her flat, a film that also looks forward to the later 'apartment' films of the 1990s and developing Akerman's persistent interest in the topographies of living and their internal contradictions.

The *Handbook* as aide-mémoire vividly draws attention to the way that the Akerman theme of collective memory develops across her later work. Commentaries on *Golden Eighties* dwell, quite correctly, on the film's cinephilic celebration of its lineage, its descent from Hollywood musicals through to Godard's *Une Femme est une femme* and to Jacques Demy's *Les Parapluies de Cherbourg* and *Les Demoiselles de Rochefort*. And Ginette Vincendeau points out (in an excerpted text) that *Nuit et Jour* in 1991 makes an important cinephile tribute to the French school of 1920s and 30s and the place of Paris as location, or even character, in their films. But these collective cinephile memories find much deeper significance in Akerman's reflections on and tributes to her own Jewish culture. While there are occasional implicit and explicit references to Jewish culture and the Holocaust in the 70s films, Akerman's first film on the subject was *Dis-moi*, a 1980 television commission for a series on grandmothers in which she interviewed elderly women Holocaust survivors, recording their thoughts and their memories. This film, unseen since it was first broadcast, is one of the most important of the retrospective's discoveries and the nearly extinct Yiddish songs sung by the participants are published in original and translation in the *Handbook*. One of Adam's most powerful blogs is about this film. He says:

'But genocide is about something else too, it is about the disruption of what it is that a mother gives her child, which is the living truth, the words, the stories and a manual for life that embodies morals, precepts and principles. Everything that defines a culture. What we have here is a redefinition of the meaning of genocide seen in terms of what lies behind a person, what is inherent in lost lives lived and what has been lived through by the survivors.'

Akerman turned to Jewish collective culture in *Histoires d'Amérique* (1989), a tribute to jokes and anecdotes as a means of survival in hard times but also as an instance of the survival of Jewish memory against all odds.

But the central work of this period, to my mind, is *D'Est*, made in 1993 and the first of her works to be exhibited in a gallery space. Shot in Poland, the DDR and the former Soviet Union, the film intertwines various differing kinds of stillness and movement: static portrait shots of individual people in their interior locations are juxtaposed with exteriors filled with movement. With *D'Est* Akerman returns to her family's pre-Holocaust origins in Eastern Europe and, perhaps only incidentally, she found in the groups of people waiting, queuing in the street, standing in railway stations, a trace or memory of the transportation of Jews to the concentration camps. There is an extraordinary synchronicity between the film's elegiac atmosphere and its investment in the cinematic: streets in the dawn snow, trains crossing paths, tram lights moving through the night and so on. In the gallery installation, the Akerman theme of seriality and sequence expands into a new dimension: the spectator moves through the serial arrangement of monitors, then stops to watch the sequence of shots on their screens, echoing the film's choreography of movement and stillness. Filmed on 16mm, displayed digitally in the gallery, capturing a cross-roads moment for both history and cinema, *D'Est* is Akerman's central, ground-breaking film of the 1990s, the film that, in the 1980s, *Golden Eighties* failed to be but that, in the 1970s, *Jeanne Dielman* had been.

D'Est prefigures Akerman's later films of landscape and political desolation: *Sud* in 1999 and *De l'autre côté* in 2002, both addressing deeply rooted instances of American racism and haunted by its dead. In 2006 she shot footage in Israel that contributed to *Là-bas*. These extraordinary, innovative uses of landscape as witness to politics, and her experimentation with new forms of gallery exhibition, are interspersed with her mature feature films: *Un Divan à New York* (1996), *La Captive* (2000) and *Demain on déménage* (2004). These features are all, in rather different ways, 'apartment' films and rework some of Akerman's earlier themes around intrusion and confinement. *Demain on déménage* beautifully evokes both Akerman's longstanding investment in the mother-daughter relationship and her love of tableaux-style narrative as a series of prospective buyers inspect their flat to crazy comic effect.

It is both appropriate and tragic that Akerman's last film would be the portrait of her mother, Natalia, a Holocaust survivor who always wanted to shield her children from the horrors of the past. *No Home Movie* was shot largely in Natalia's flat in Brussels, but also intercuts Skype conversations conducted during Akerman's many travels and footage of the desert landscape of Israel. The film also reflects Akerman's idea of herself as a nomad who always returned to her mother. Her struggles with depression and insomnia were well known in film circles; many of her friends thought that she would not survive her mother's inevitable death. We have to be extremely grateful that she still had the indomitable courage to make this final film. She said:

'Even if I have a home in Paris and sometimes in New York, whenever I was saying I have to go home, it was going to my mother,' 'And there is 'no home' anymore, because she isn't there, and when I came the last time, the home was empty.'

This tragic context gives the retrospective, as recorded in the *Handbook*, particular resonance. Its diligence and care stand as a real and material tribute to Akerman's films, made across forty years of all too short a life. To reiterate my early points: the *Handbook* captures something of the vitality that Akerman invested in her films, her uncompromising originality and her extraordinary ability to conjure up the magical power of cinema. But as a collage of writing of many different kinds, the *Handbook* crucially bears witness to the effect that Akerman has had on the film community, from her earliest movies until her last. The presence of Akerman scholars and aficionados who introduced the screenings, the high quality of the texts included in the book are all a reminder of the way that her 'cinematic' qualities have advanced our understanding of film. I would like to draw attention to Adam Roberts's wonderful blogs, mini-essays, that shift elegantly between critical perceptions, personal feelings and important factual notes. Altogether, the *Handbook* has too many important and useful features to enumerate here.

Most of all, whether she would like it or not, Chantal Akerman undoubtedly created a women's cinema. Her films have a way of holding back the forward propulsion of time, whether through elegant serial patterns or the wit of narrative indecision. Her intuitive and poetic understanding of feminine space was always subjected to a rigorously contradictory spirit: to be exploded in

Saute ma ville or treasured and celebrated in *No Home Movie*. But out of a woman's way of envisaging and experiencing the world, she turned cinema upside down, with stories and images of a kind never seen or told before. And I welcome the *Chantal Akerman Retrospective Handbook* as an imaginative and important contribution to this legacy.

Introduction

A RETROSPECTIVE OF the films and videos of Chantal Akerman was presented in London between 2013 and 2015, curated by *A Nos Amours*, an independent curation and programming project founded by Joanna Hogg and Adam Roberts.

This introduction will set out a brief history of *A Nos Amours*, its ambitions and raison d'être, then describe the circumstances of the retrospective and related events.

Overall, the purpose of this book is to share the written materials that supported the retrospective, and to share accurate and useful details about the individual films and video works so that other curators, programmers and anyone otherwise interested will have easy access to what is currently not so easily to hand, at least in English. It may even serve to draw attention to lesser-known works in Akerman's oeuvre that deserve attention.

A BRIEF HISTORY OF A NOS AMOURS

WE WERE LUCKY to have discovered cinema at a time when repertory cinemas provided lovingly curated film programmes, whose tickets were cheap by any standards, and which repeated a large number of the canonical works of world cinema. It was possible to sit all day in a cinema if life allowed, and so scoop up much of any given film-maker's oeuvre within a year or two. The BBC and then Channel 4 also devoted prime-time slots to great films diligently presented and advocated. It was not so rare to see work by Bresson, Ozu, Rossellini, Mizoguchi, or Tarkovsky on prime-time TV, for free. Those days, in so many ways, are gone. Having taught film directing at Central Saint

Martins it was plain to us that next generations of film-makers and new audiences simply did not have that bedrock of film viewing. Their references were relatively recent and tended to the mainstream. It was clear that if we had been handed such a flame we should at least try to pass it on.

Another coincidence, that quickened out thinking, was our discovering that we had both, by sheer coincidence, been watching films of Maurice Pialat. That is to say, we had both been watching DVDs alone in our respective homes. It is far from ideal to see cinema films on a small screen, without an audience to share the time with. Something fundamental about the potential of film had been lost. We concluded that if we wanted to see these films as a member of an audience, on a decent screen (as must have been assumed by all film-makers until recent times), then we might have to organise screenings ourselves.

The fate of repertory cinema is not important to look into here, although the obstacles we faced when proposing to present our first screenings in 2011 perhaps illuminate what had happened.

To begin with there is now a severe shortage of prints in good condition. Most prints were made long ago and have exceeded their expected life span. We have run prints reeking of vinegar and falling apart, likely to be their last time passing through a projector. No new prints are being made. And even if good prints are located, the cost of shipping, and the fees payable to the archives that store them, are not insignificant. Moreover, few cinemas are ready and able to deal with a shrunken, aged print. If a print belongs to an archive, then there are very few cinemas approved to run their precious prints.

But the biggest obstacle by far is the cost of theatrical licence. If the rights owner is Gaumont, for example, the cost is fixed, high and non-negotiable. Such rights owners are content for a film never to play rather than to offer an economic rental. If the rights owner is Mosfilm then we might fail simply because there was a new chilling of relations between the UK and Russia. If the rights owner is a major studio then a one-off screening is simply of no interest at all to them and so permission is refused (James Gray's unseen *The Immigrant* is an example).

We were proposing one-off screenings, with no guarantee of a sell-out audience. Rights owners generally want a guaranteed minimum. We had therefore to accept significant risk.

Some cinemas, happily, were kind enough to offer us slots in return for a share of the box office. But we had to cover the cost of the film from our portion alone. The challenge was immense, not least with cinema membership schemes meaning that a share of box office is of far less value than the audience numbers might suggest. The economics of this kind of screening are far from easy.

We decided that the risks could be managed, simply by scaling the screenings to match the potential revenues. If there were a handful of people to start with then we would screen films for which we could find a decent DVD and hope for the kindness of rights owners. This is what happened. As we gathered a social media following and built a respectable mailing list we were able to be much more ambitious. We moved quickly towards screening the best possible copy in the best possible location. Happily, audiences chose to attend and we were able to share in some really truly wonderful screenings. We often asked people to raise hands if they had not seen a film before – many hands would often be raised. We were reaching the people we had hoped to reach. Tarkovsky was far from new to us, yet it was unknown territory to many hand-raisers. Perhaps the flame was guttering slightly less uncertainly.

The strategy needed to make the screenings work seemed obvious to us: make them exciting events. We invited the great and the good to introduce films. We drew on all our friends and colleagues to use their social media clout to get the screenings talked about. We pestered the few remaining listings services. We developed a solid mailing list.

The venues were varied, as we did not want to become
identified with any one physical location. The ideal was
the sheer excitement of seeing films sitting among other
excitable and interested people. The introductions were
not to be expert lectures; they had to be above all passionate
advocacy. Ideally, speakers knew and loved the films they
were talking about. Excitement is infectious, as we quickly
learned. Many of the films we programmed were obscure.
Fred Kelemen's *Frost*, for example, was shown from a
16mm cutting copy because no final print existed. It runs
at 270 minutes.

AN AKERMAN RETROSPECTIVE

A NOS AMOURS was founded with a commitment that women
film-makers would be represented equally. In 2013 we had
failed to do that. Only one film by a woman had been included
(and even then this was *Chronik der Anna Magdalena Bach*,
co-directed by Danièle Huillet with a man), despite our every
effort. We had researched films by Larisa Shepitko but the prints
proved unobtainable. We researched films by Margaret Tait, but
news came of a retrospective elsewhere. We wanted to show
films by Joan Micklin Silver but shipping rare prints from the US
was impossibly expensive.

Chantal Akerman was known to us, because she enjoyed
a good reputation and we had been able to see a few of her
films. It was, however, surprising to discover that there had
been no recent retrospective and that much of her work had
never been shown in the UK, despite a great deal interest from
film-makers, feminists, academics and film theorists. Initial
enquiries showed that the work was not available from any
one source, and that good copies might be hard to locate. The
Cinémathèque Royale in Brussels had prints of the feature

films and some shorts, but some were in poor condition. Many were not subtitled. They had undertaken some digitising of the 1970s films (a DVD box set was available), but there was no current programme of restoration.

Happily, Lore Gablier at Akerman's production company Paradise Films offered to support our proposal to present a retrospective in London. Lore gave us many necessary leads and introductions, not least to the TV companies that had funded a number of films and still controlled rights. Finding the correct contact (*le responsable*) in multinational media companies was nevertheless far from easy.

Worst of all, many films had never been translated and subtitled. To proceed with a retrospective seemed impossible, yet to us clearly imperative.

A SLOW RETROSPECTIVE

A NOS AMOURS had been accustomed to present one a film a month, sometimes less than that. This gave time for preparation, for planning ahead, and for social media campaigning that might connect with the potential audience for each event. This rhythm suited us also because we had other work to do. If we undertook a retrospective, we saw no reason to accelerate or to bunch up the screenings, as is the norm when a cinémathèque presents a director season (in London's BFI Southbank as much as anywhere). A slow retrospective seemed like a novel and interesting idea. It would give time to digest work, to follow the development of a film practice in something more like real time.

Moreover, the work needed to locate copies, translate and subtitle them would not be insignificant, not least for a group of volunteers working in their spare time.

IT WAS NECESSARY to find a venue for the retrospective – one that could deal with all formats, including 16mm, 35mm, digital and DCP[1]. We would need to be able to present films with live subtitles, as projected text superimposed onto the film image. We needed a reasonable box office agreement. We needed visionary commitment. When we met Jo Blair, who worked for Picturehouse and programmed the cinema at the Institute of Contemporary Arts (ICA), we found just that. Jo was able to offer terms that gave us that chance. Moreover, Jo turned out to be one of the most loyal members of the audience. We salute Jo Blair, an exemplary and wonderful collaborator. James King, in his capacity as cinema manager at ICA, wholeheartedly committed his institution to the project, offering access to the ICA blogging (now called *Bulletin*), and agreed to include the screenings in ICA mailouts.

Having secured ICA Cinema as partner, we were able to ask for support from the BFI Programming Development Fund (specifically the Audience Fund 2013 – 17). This fund was created to support just our sort of collaborative project. Securing their financial support meant that we could proceed with confidence. Another source of funding was a grant from Wallonie-Bruxelles International (WBI). Later on, we were also able to secure a grant from Film London's *Boost* scheme, to support events such as the mid-retrospective symposium (see Chapter 8). We now felt confident that our proposal was a realistic and costed one.

Contacting Chantal Akerman herself we found her approachable and happy with the proposals. Her intervention with the Cinémathèque Royale de Belgique secured agreement to borrow their prints, at a good price.

All the same, the search for the work not readily accessible via Paradise Films was incredibly demanding. It entailed, for example, tracking down executives at TV companies, who had the

1. DCP is a Digital Cinema Package, the current format for digital cinema

authority to grant access to work that the company simply did not normally distribute. There are no accessible directories for staff at such companies, and so the search was sometimes frustrating. Even if we found the right executive, the copy of the programme would not necessarily be found via that person, and so the search would have to begin again. Some institutions were underfunded and so what materials they had were in poor condition and not well conserved. Hoarders of prints were a sometimes helpful source of materials. We began our retrospective not sure it could be complete. It was by now very clear why there has not yet been another complete retrospective.

VOLUNTEERS

A NOS AMOURS was founded as a volunteer-run project. We have always sought to meet expenses or provide per diems if possible, but ours was a project defined above all by enthusiasm and love of the work that we wanted to screen. A group of exceptionally committed and brilliant volunteers gathered to work on the retrospective. It is a pleasure to recite their names (in alphabetical order):

Chahine Fellahi, Jessica Fletcher, Rosie Goddard, Kim Goldsmith, Ella Harris, Eve Marguerite, Ioana Salagean and Keifer Taylor.

Live subtitling and much of the translating by Charlotte Maconochie was done to a very high standard and with marvellous attention to nuance. Her live cueing of subtitles for *Letters Home* in particular – where dialogue is delivered at breakneck speed for 104 minutes – was seamless and virtuoso. Impossible not to have thought the subtitles burned into the print.

The projectionists at ICA Cinema dealt wonderfully with the bizarre mix of formats. Live subtitles were a challenge, as we had no access to professional equipment – and so we had to devise ways of doing this, using PowerPoint slides and video projectors. There were occasions when the technical problems almost overwhelmed us.

Translation was done for the most part by Charlotte Maconochie, though a few others also provided translation. They are: Sylvie Beaufils, Louise Lyon, Oenone Dudley, Penny Averill and Adam Roberts. Akerman's made-for-TV documentary *Dis-moi* (1980) was an extraordinary exception. This film includes a song sung in Yiddish, a dialect of Yiddish that the Holocaust has made tragically rare indeed. A network of connections led us to Rabbi Jeremy Rosen in New York who was able to give us the final translation. It was the work of several hands to produce the finished English-language text. Our translations and subtitle sets for *Dis-moi* and others have now been used for screenings all over the world.

INTRODUCTIONS

AS HAS BEEN said, *A Nos Amours* invariably invites guest speakers to give introductions to the screenings. Our approach for this retrospective would be no different. We asked those who had long been champions of Akerman's work. Laura Mulvey, for example, was responsible for the first UK screenings of Akerman's films at the Edinburgh International Film Festival, and we were delighted therefore that she introduced *Jeanne Dielman*. But we were keen also to cast our net as widely as possible. Thus, for example, artist Lucy Cash spoke before the screenings of *Un Jour Pina a demandé*, *A Nos Amours* volunteer Keifer Taylor introduced *D'Est*, producer and television commissioner John Ellis introduced Akerman's *Family Business*, novelist and film-maker Xiaolu Guo introduced *News from home*, and Akerman's long-time friend and collaborator Claire Atherton introduced *Letters Home*. The complete list of speakers appears in the appendix.

THE HAND OUTS

IT HAS BEEN our practice to provide a printed take away A4 sheet at screenings, that provides a list of credits, and perhaps reference to useful texts to read either before or after seeing the film. This was also a space to share translations or useful transcriptions. This practice was adopted for the retrospective. This book provides permanent access to what we shared or recommended. The credits, as far as we have been able to determine, are accurate and checked by several of Akerman's colleagues.

BLOGGING/SOCIAL MEDIA

IN PRESENTING THIS retrospective, we did not want only to attract an audience of aficionados. We wanted to reach those who had not heard of Akerman, or simply not found an opportunity to see the work. And we wanted those who had never sat in an auditorium to see these films and so discover what can happen when films are watched collectively.

It was therefore necessary to develop in our billings, posting and mailouts a growing sense of the purpose of the work, its formal qualities and its specific virtue. The task was to engage, to catch a casual reader's eye and ear. It was important to strike the right balance between underlining the emotional satisfaction to be hoped for if watching the films, as well as register their standing as beacons for feminists, film theorists and cinephiles. It seemed important to deploy only as much theoretical insight as might support and animate the promised experience, for this was not to be a retrospective offered in an academic institution. By the same token, we could not sell the project too cheaply as the work is subtle and profound. Ideally, if this promotion were to be done well, then new viewers may take a risk.

The challenge was not a simple one. Akerman's films range from four minutes in duration to more than three hours. The films may be comedies, musicals, narratives or documentaries. What could possibly connect such diversity? What will reward one viewer without potentially alienating another? Why would a series of 25 screenings be worth anybody's time or shilling?

A series of blogs and articles were written for the *A Nos Amours* blog, the ICA website and *Huffington Post* (*HuffPo*). New content was promoted by means of social media – Twitter and Facebook. Gradually a critical mass of followers and readers were gathered, which converted into improving attendances, and an audience willing to take a risk. Numbers grew and then stabilised. We exceeded our predictions. Crucially, we were financially secure, and did not lose money. These blog posts are included in the book. So, too, are articles for *The Guardian* and *Frieze* magazine, written after Chantal Akerman's death.

THE LAUNCH 26 September 2013

WE DECIDED THAT the films should ideally play in the order in which they were made. We wanted to travel through the work, in Akerman's footsteps, able to sense how her restless energies flowed first in one direction and then in another.

The retrospective launched at ICA Cinema on Thursday 26 September 2013. We screened Akerman's first three films, including a great rarity: *L'Enfant aimé – ou je joue à être une femme mariée* (1971). Because this was to be a complete retrospective Akerman exceptionally consented to this film being shown. Akerman had expressed critical feelings about the film (she had termed it 'a failure') and had all but suppressed it, though she extracted a shot from it to make the installation artwork *Dans le miroir* (2007). The film, screened from a 16mm print, required translation and subtitling, with subtitles cued live. A blog piece makes a case for the film and is included in this book.

AKERMAN IN PERSON

NATURALLY WE HOPED that Akerman would attend a screening, which she did on Thursday 22 May 2014. The programme on this occasion paired *Un Jour Pina a demandé* (1983) and *L'Homme à la valise* (1983). The artist Lucy Cash had introduced the first film, when Akerman arrived. The capacity audience jumped to its feet to offer a standing ovation. Following the second film, Akerman entered into a lively and memorable impromptu dialogue with the audience. The ICA recorded this encounter and an audio file can be found on *A Nos Amours* SoundCloud page, a link to which is provided on our website.

A MID-RETROSPECTIVE SYMPOSIUM 12 October 2014

THE SLOW RETROSPECTIVE would last two years, which is a long haul. As we reached the mid-point, it seemed right to gather and talk about impressions and expectations. Academics who have written on Akerman's work gave papers, but we devoted time to look at work from emerging film-makers and artists who claim Akerman as a touchstone. We were delighted that Akerman decided to join us for the day.

JW3 on Finchley Road in London provided the venue and generous hospitality.

The day began with a video of Akerman interviewing her mother Natalia, recorded in 2007.

Academics Sarah Pucill, Griselda Pollock, Muriel Tinel-Temple and Alison Rowley gave papers.

The films and artworks, curated by *A Nos Amours* volunteer
Eve Marguerite, were by Amber Jacobs (*Curds and Whey*, 2013),
Pia Ilonka (*Little Short Film*, 2015), Rebecca Aldridge (images
and text) and Amy Croft (*grey sky blue*, 2012).

In a booklet for the event we were pleased to publish writing
by Isabel Taube on *Jeanne Dielman*, written under Oulipian
constraints while she was enrolled on the Royal College of Art
Critical Writing MA.

A video of Akerman's extended Q&A chaired by Dr Alison
Rowley was recorded and will be made available online, via the
A Nos Amours website.

JE TU IL ELLE – A NATIONAL RELEASE 17 March 2015

JO BLAIR OF Picturehouse Cinemas came to us with a
proposal: would we like to pick a film to play across f the
Picturehouse chain nationally, as part of what they call *Discover
Tuesday*? The films programmed in this way tend to be valuable
but marginal, picked because they deserve to be more widely
seen. We proposed *je tu il elle* (1974). Akerman was supportive,
and gave us the go-ahead to make digital copies to send to the
participating cinemas. The film rights belonged to Paradise
Films. The Cinémathèque Royale in Brussels declined to
support this proposal, and so we were obliged to make do with
a less than ideal video file. Akerman assured us she was happy
even if we were far from content ourselves! A few independent
cinemas joined the scheme. Tuesday 17 March 2015 was the
date selected.

We made a trailer which ran in Picturehouse cinemas for a
month beforehand (this trailer can be seen via our website).
Some cinemas booked introductions. At Brighton's Duke of
York's, for example, which sold out, John David Rhodes (a film
scholar now at Cambridge) introduced.

We issued a call for supportive statements, which Picturehouse graphic artists turned into beautiful jpegs to tweet and post. The statements were:

It's stark, hypnotic and completely unforgettable (Richard Kwietniowski); When I watch Akerman I am always surprised there aren't more women directors (Chris Petit); Akerman portrays woman with woman with a casual intensity rarely seen on the screen (Lisa Appignanesi); Her movies give cinema heft (Mark Cousins); Simply, Chantal Akerman is the supreme autobiographer of the cinema (Paul Mayersberg)

That day, more than 2,400 people saw *je tu il elle*.

BREAK-OUT SCREENINGS

AS THE RETROSPECTIVE proceeded, and our social media followers and the mailing list grew to include followers all over Britain and the world, we began to receive several enquiries from people outside London longing to see Akerman's films. Being a volunteer grouping, we could only offer to help clear rights and locate screening copies. It was with great delight that as a result in Glasgow, at CCA in June 2014, three programmes of films by Akerman were programmed by local artist Sacha Airlie. Following this there were screenings also in Leeds and Bristol. None of these received financial support from any funder or agency.

NO HOME MOVIE – AKERMAN'S FINAL FILM

AKERMAN FILMED WHAT would become *No Home Movie* in the course of 2013 and 2014. Her subject was her own mother, Natalia, a Holocaust survivor, and a figure of towering importance in Akerman's life and work. Sadly, Natalia, aged

86, died shortly after filming, lending an already poignant and tender portrayal an additional freight of emotional power.

We did not know, as we secured agreement to screen this film, the 25th in our retrospective, that it was to be Akerman's last work. At the time, we were simply delighted to be closing with Akerman's brand new film for cinema. The screening was scheduled for 30 October 2015.

Indeed, in order that the film be distributed in the UK, so that audiences outside London might see it, we entered into an agreement with Contemporary Films to distribute the film. Also, as a result of this distribution, a deal for screening on UK television was secured, which has meant that the film has been shown on the Channel 4's Film4 Channel.

AKERMAN IS DEAD 5 October 2015

ON THIS DAY Chantal Akerman killed herself. Her sister Sylviane informed *Libération* and it was their front page that revealed the shocking news to the world. Social media carried the ill tidings to us all.

In terms of the retrospective, the penultimate screening, of *La Folie Almayer* (2011), was scheduled to take place on 22 October. This screening was suddenly and shockingly therefore to be a posthumous screening. Gregor Muir, then Director of the ICA, gave an address, as did Claire Atherton, who came especially from Paris for the occasion. We added a brief introduction to the film. *La Folie Almayer* is Akerman's adaptation of Joseph Conrad's story. The film deals with the collapse into madness of a mind fragmented by the impossibility of the post-colonial morass, with its burden of despair. It seemed appropriate.

AKERMAN NOW – THE INSTALLATION WORKS

WE WERE WELL aware that Akerman had been making installation artwork since 1995. Two of these works had been shown at Camden Arts Centre in London in 2008. Antwerp had seen a very large show in 2012. The work made use of moving images, often culled from her single-screen work. We wanted to see how Akerman's gallery practice connected with and perhaps illuminated what she had done in the cinema. The only way to find out was to organise an exhibition. That thought had presented itself more and more compellingly as the retrospective progressed. Each time we met with Akerman, the installation work was mentioned, for it was by now a significant part of her practice. By the time of the mid-retrospective symposium, the idea was fully formed. We would try to find a way to bring a large-scale exhibition work to London. The retrospective would come to embrace all her practice.

This idea would become the *Akerman NOW* show at Ambika P3, which is not the subject of this book, as its preparation and presentation were a separate venture, funded by the Arts Council England, with Akerman's direct involvement in its planning and design (this work done in the year prior to her death).

The show opened with a private view on 29 October 2015. It was timed to coincide with the final screening of *No Home Movie*, closing the retrospective on 30th October 2015 at Regent Street Cinema, a venue attached to Ambika P3 (both being part of the University of Westminster), and within walking distance of each other.

THE SCREENING OF *No Home Movie* had been planned
to be the happy end of the retrospective, a gala event
that would launch Akerman's arriving in London to
open the exhibition at Ambika P3, and to precede an
unprecedented masterclass that she had agreed to give.
We would also have been announcing an international
academic conference devoted to Akerman's work. The
news of her death changed everything.

To begin with, the screening would now be a memorial event.
Akerman's sister Sylviane attended, and saw the film, in which
she appears, for the first time. Akerman's childhood friend
Marilyn Watelet also attended. Claire Atherton, who had edited
the film, delivered a homily. A capacity audience at Regent Street
Cinema shared in their tears.

The masterclass, a first for Akerman, was to have been given
on 31 October. London would have been truly blessed.

AFTERWARDS

WE HAD PROPOSED, at meetings in 2014 with the University
of Westminster's Centre for Research and Education in Arts and
Media, that we might convene a conference to bring academic
perspectives to bear on Akerman's work, as a way to round off
the retrospective. Professor Rosie Thomas offered full support,
and indeed it was she who suggested Ambika P3 as collaborator
for the installation exhibition.

However, given Akerman's sudden death, the conference was
delayed, becoming eventually *After Chantal: An International
Conference*, which took place in London between 4 and
6 November 2016. This was attended by leading Akerman
scholars from all over the world.

This book is an outcome of the retrospective, a rounding off. But it is not alone. Publication coincides with an edition of the journal MIRAJ dedicated to writing on Akerman, some of it arising from the conference. A book titled *Afterlives*, from the academic imprint Legenda, edited by Professors Marion Schmid and Emma Wilson, is also published at this time, containing writing about Akerman and her legacy.

All these connect via the retrospective screenings, at which over the two years of its course a community formed, interested in the work, transformed by her work, and (pace Levinas) were made morally better by her work.

It is a matter of astonishment to us that we were able to present in London what to this day is the only complete retrospective of Akerman's film and video work. Akerman's help was critical in this regard, because she was able to help us resolve difficulties, and supply introductions where needed.

We discovered that no one film of hers is any less worth knowing than another, because Akerman's tireless and questioning mind never rested. She changed idiom and manner frequently, in order that she avoid the pitfall of repetition. Her tireless quest for new forms was an abiding aspect of her project. As she complained, to have already made a masterpiece at such a young age was both a curse and a challenge.

The challenge for those of us who remain is to continue to look at the work and think about the work, and above all share the work.

ACKNOWLEDGMENTS – AND A HOPE

FOLLOWING AKERMAN'S DEATH, a foundation has been established by Akerman's heir Sylviane Akerman, to whom we are very much indebted for permission to quote Akerman's words in this book.

But this book would also not have been possible were it not also for invaluable help and support from Marilyn Watelet and Claire Atherton, Akerman's life-long friends and frequent collaborators. Babette Mangolte also provided invaluable and detailed recollection. Such help in gathering and fact-checking will mean this handbook will hopefully prove to be a reliable and useful sourcebook.

We also wish to thank the myriad friends of Akerman, and the community that sprang up around her work. We have compiled for the close of this book a list of those with whom we came into contact in the course of this retrospective. There will inevitably be regrettable omissions, and we apologise for that. We would have liked to include a list of everyone who bought a ticket, since without that simple gesture this retrospective would have failed. Therefore, to everyone who attended, thank you.

We can only hope that Akerman's work will continue to be available and visible – it is worrying that relatively few screenings have taken place worldwide since the terrible day in 2015 when film-making lost one of its most important and radical voices. We call on the Cinémathèque Royale de Belgique and its director, who have been granted a duty of care, to make the films easily and economically available to be seen. The silencing of women is a theme Akerman explored and exposed, and it would be a tragedy if that silencing were to be extended to her after death.

The screenings

AKERMAN I TO AKERMAN 26

IN WHAT FOLLOWS, we reprint the billings, paper hand-outs prepared for each screening and any other materials that may not be available elsewhere. The billings were sent out by email and also appeared on the *A Nos Amours* and ICA websites. The paper hand-outs were given out at screenings, as a souvenir of the event, providing a record of important credits, translations as necessary, or else reading suggestions. For this publication we reproduce these hand-outs, with some inadvertent factual errors and omissions corrected.

A note regarding film titles: *A Nos Amours* has tended to make use of original languge titles, providing translated titles if relevant, for example, *Demain on déménage* (*Tommorow We Move*). Regarding capitalisation of French names of films, we have adopted for this publication the Bon Usage rules (thus *Ecrire contre l'oubli*), unless the title as presented in the film itself seemed worth preserving, as for example *je tu il elle* or *News from home*.

Akerman 1

THE FIRST THREE FILMS

BILLING

A Nos Amours commences a complete retrospective of Chantal Akerman's entire cinematic oeuvre, beginning with Akerman's first three films, including the beguiling, beautiful, rigorous *Hotel Monterey*, and the film that launched the career of Chantal Akerman, *Saute ma Ville*.

Saute ma Ville (1968, 13')
L'Enfant aimé – ou je joue à être une femme mariée
(1971, 35')
Hotel Monterey (1972, 63')

Introduced by Nina Danino (artist film-maker and Reader in Fine Art at Goldsmiths, University of London)

Akerman's work has consistently offered a playful and beguiling critique of cinema. Over a vast and hugely varied body of work, Akerman has brilliantly energised the avant-garde project, personalising and humanising the dead spaces created by consumerism and the habitual lives we inhabit.

Akerman's cinema goes far beyond popular notions of image making, beyond modernist and feminist strategies, in pursuit of her obsession with borders, with the tension between documentary and fiction, between her mother and herself, between chaos and control, cinema and history.

BLOGGING

In defence of Akerman's *L'Enfant aimé*

ICA Bulletin, 27 November 2013, see page 173.

THE HAND-OUT

Akerman 1: the first three films

Thursday 26 September 2013. ICA Cinema, 7.30pm. Introduced by Nina Danino.

Chantal Akerman was born 6th June 1950 in Brussels. Her parents were Jews who survived the Holocaust. Her life has been one of movement, migration and exploration of margins and borders. Her body of work includes features, documentary and installation work. A Nos Amours intends to screen all her surviving film work for cinema.

L'Enfant aimé – ou je joue à être une femme mariée

(*The Beloved Child, or I play at being a married woman*) With: Chantal Akerman, Claire Wauthion and Daphné Merzer; 1971 16mm b&w 35'; Live subtitles translated by Charlotte Maconochie and Penny Averill, cued by Charlotte Maconochie.

Saute ma ville

(*Blow Up My Town*) With: Chantal Akerman; Camera: René Fruchter; Assistant director: Richard Bréchet; Editing: Geneviève Luciani; Sound recording: Patrice. 1968 35mm b&w 13'.

Hotel Monterey

Camera: Babette Mangolte; Editing: Geneviève Luciani; 1972 16mm colour 63'.

Melissa Anderson: Why did you move to New York?
Chantal Akerman: I moved because I had a strange but realistic feeling that things were happening here. I was 18 when I left Brussels; I went to Paris, then after Paris I spent six months in Jerusalem. My father wanted me to get married, married, married. I did one film, *Saute ma ville* (1968), that was really good but then I did a second film that was very bad. I thought I was lucky, like when you play cards for the first time, but since the second film was very bad, it meant I'd better do what my parents wanted me to do: get married. But it was like a denial of myself. I had known a man – he's since died of AIDS – ever since I was a child; he was in Jerusalem and we decided to

get married. But after a few months in Jerusalem, I got very bored. I said, "Why don't we go to New York? I think it's there, something's in the air." I was 21, he was 22. We arrived with 50 bucks in our pocket.

MA: And you arrived in 1971?

CA: Yes. I had the telephone number of Babette Mangolte [who would become the cinematographer for several of Akerman's films, including *Jeanne Dielman*], through a film-maker that knew her. And I don't know why I called her, because I don't call so much. But I did, and there was a beautiful voice, answering me. I did not know this, but she was into the most revolutionary art world at the moment, that maybe only 500 were into. It was Richard Serra, Annette Michelson from NYU, Jonas Mekas, all the people from the Anthology Film Archives, Richard Foreman. All those people were totally revolutionary, and I was a little girl who didn't know anything. I showed to Jonas *Saute ma ville*, and he loved it. So I was immediately part of the family. And I discovered another way of looking at things. So, I was right to come here, but if I didn't know Babette, how would I have known that I should go to Anthology Film Archives or to look at [plays by] Richard Foreman? I had never heard those names, you know? Babette's still in my life now, so it's great.

MA: How long did you live in New York?

CA: I stayed from November '71 to maybe April '73. But in the meantime, I went back to Europe for two to three months to edit *Hotel Monterey* and *La Chambre*. I did another film that I lost; almost all the footage was about kids who were in rehabilitation and prevention programmes in Yonkers. We were shooting in reversal at the time, so we had no negative. I lost half, three-quarters of it, but you know, I was like a vagabond with my film.

(From *Her Brilliant Decade*, an interview with Chantal Akerman, by Melissa Anderson found at *www.movingimagesource.us*. Melissa Anderson is the film editor of 4Columns. Thanks for permission to reprint.)

MISCELLANEOUS

L'Enfant aimé – ou je joue à être une femme mariée was
translated and subtitled for this screening, as far as we are
aware for the first time. A full subtitle list is available from
A Nos Amours.

Three extracts, including the scene which Akerman used for
her gallery work *Dans le miroir* (a woman assessing her own
body, and naming its parts):

1

I really love him so much – he's such a boy
You wouldn't think it to look at him
He's a real baby
Even...
Even in sex, he's a real baby
Well, at times he's like a baby
And that's quite nice
At first...
I imagined, when we first met,
that I would do anything to please him
In the end, I realised...
At home, I sometimes felt like
his mother, which annoyed me at first...
That's normal, don't you think?
He's really lovely with Daphna.

2

At the beginning, I thought we'd make love
all the time, all the time...
I didn't realise that that would stop
It's difficult for me that his job
is so important to him...
sometimes more important than me
I was waiting at home all day,

waiting for him to come back...
... and I must get over it
Sometimes I was hysterical
I'm ashamed to talk about it
I ran around outside in the pouring rain.
I was mad.
And for him, he was annoyed to see me like that,
he was frightened...
...and felt that he had to make love to me
Little by little, it calmed down
Now, I think I love him more
I used to think that I could leave him,
before we had Daphna
Now, sometimes I get depressed
I can't bear even the ticking sound of a clock,
a church bell...
I feel my time is completely useless
I can do whatever I want,
arrange the house exactly as I wish
Buy anything I want

3

I'm pale
I have a long neck
I'm not as tall as I look
because I have long arms
long legs
and a small face
I have freckles
I have a pretty mouth
I have almost no waist
I have a very curved back
I'm pale
My ears stick out a little

I have wrinkles
My belly sticks out if I don't hold it in
I have delicate wrists…
I've got almost no bust
I've got one shoulder
lower than the other
And a long neck
My eyes are the same colour
as my hair
I've got a hairy chin
I have a little nose
I have a big arse…
…a bit of cellulite
My stomach sticks out
I'm going to the window

(Translation Penny Averill and Charlotte Maconochie)

Akerman 2

TWO SHORTS & *JE TU IL ELLE*

BILLING

A Nos Amours continues a retrospective of the complete
film works of Chantal Akerman, with two short films and her
breakthrough feature-length film of 1972 *je tu il elle*.

Chantal Akerman is a film-maker whose time has
come. Akerman's work is superficially wide-ranging – spanning
documentary and narrative, film and video, 16mm and 35mm,
cinema and art gallery – and yet her work is characterised by an
uncompromising and singular sense of purpose.

What Akerman shows us, by means structural and otherwise,
is nothing less than the human condition, a series of
astonishing mediations on loneliness and anxiety, alienation
and discomfort. She began inspired by Godard, but quickly
established a startling and provocative project that is among
the very greatest in European film. As J Hoberman has said:
'Comparable in force and originality to Godard or Fassbinder,
Chantal Akerman is arguably the most important European
director of her generation'.

La Chambre (1972, 11')
Le 15/8 (1973, 42')
je tu il elle (1975, 86')

Mark Cousins: Powell and Pressburger once wrote 'no true artist
believes in escapism.' They could have been writing about the films
of Chantal Akerman. Her movies give cinema heft. They have the
rigour of a Poussin painting. She looks longer and harder than most
directors, and almost seems to stop film's flicker. (email to *A Nos Amours*)

Akerman 2: two shorts & *je tu il elle*

Thursday 28 November 2013. ICA Cinema, 7pm.

La Chambre

With: Chantal Akerman; Camera: Babette Mangolte; Editing: Geneviève Luciani;
1972 16mm colour mute 11'.

Le 15/8

With: Chris Myllykoski; Camera: Chantal Akerman and Samy Szlingerbaum; Editing:
Chantal Akerman and Samy Szlingerbaum; Written and directed: Chantal Akerman
and Samy Szlingerbaum; 1973 16mm b&w 42'.

je tu il elle

With: Chantal Akerman, Niels Arestrup, Claire Wauthion; Screenplay: Chantal
Akerman, Eric de Kuyper, Paul Paquay; Camera: Bénédicte Delesalle; Assistants:
Charlotte Szlovak and Renelde Dupont; Editing: Luc Freché, Geneviève Luciani;
Location recording: Samy Szlingerbaum; Post-sync recording: Alain Pierre; Foley:
Marc Lobet; Re-recording mixer: Gérard Rousseau; 1975 35mm b&w 86'.

"I don't feel like I belong, and that's without real pain, without
pride. Pride happens. No, I'm just disconnected, from practically
everything. I have a few anchors, and sometimes I let them go or
they let me go, and I drift. That's most of the time. Sometimes I
hang on for a few days, minutes, seconds, then I let go again. I
can hardly look. I can hardly hear. Semi-blind, semi-deaf, I float.
Sometimes I sink. But not quite. Something, sometimes a detail,
brings me back to the surface, and I start floating again."

(From Akerman's voiceover to *Là-bas* (2006).)

Gwendolyn Audrey Foster: Born in 1950, Akerman came to the
United States after leaving films school in Belgium. One of her first
jobs was as a cashier for the 55th Street Playhouse, a porn theatre
in New York City. In an interview with Gary Indiana, Akerman
noted that, "I worked at the 55th Street Playhouse.... As a cashier;
and I amassed $4000 and made *Hotel Monterey* (1972) and *La
Chambre* (1972) with that". Claiming that she was profoundly

influenced by Jean-Luc Godard's *Pierrot le fou* (1965), Akerman established her style even in these early efforts. In *Hotel Monterey*, for example, people often move in and out of the frame of a stationary camera. Already Akerman is expressing an interest in the transient nature of modern life, with an emphatic eye towards spaces that underscore the discord of mobility – hotels, train stations – and the people who move within these spaces.

je tu il elle (1974) is Akerman's breakthrough feature-length film, composed of long blocks of static black-and-white takes, reminiscent of the films of Andy Warhol. Asked about Warhol's influence on her work, Akerman noted that she had seen only *Chelsea Girls* (1966) and *Eat* (1963), and commented that "a critic said I have something from Warhol and something from Robert Wilson, that I'm a mixture of that. Probably Warhol is a big, big originator... but I wasn't because I saw it; it was something that was there. I think my films are more sentimental". Akerman's impassive camera documents the solitary life of a single woman adrift in an industrial world. The scene of this woman, naked and alone, desperately eating sugar, is remarkable for its intensity, as is the footage of her desperately arranging and rearranging the meagre furniture in her apartment. The woman then hitchhikes, and gives an off-screen hand job to a truck driver. Feminist critics have scrutinised this scene, sometimes missing the camp humour inherent in such treatment of sexuality. Next, the woman makes love to another woman, in a sequence that has similarly attracted a great deal of attention from feminist critics. Because the camera records the action in a scientific manner, the scene has often been noted for its self-conscious display of dehumanisation and lack of visual pleasure.

However, as Andrea Weiss points out, this "absolutely un-eroticised lesbian lovemaking scene must be credited for its courage in 1974, especially given that it includes the film-maker in the scene and rejects art cinema conventions governing lesbian sexuality". The camera positioning is specifically meant to de-aestheticise the onscreen lovemaking, by making us aware of our off-screen voyeurism. The naturalistic use of sound also underscores the scene's break from Hollywood and art-house depictions of sexuality.

However, not all critics have found the scene to be without eroticism. I find the scene more erotic than conventionally constructed sex scenes because of Akerman's embrace of natural sound and image, and because of the tension that develops in watching such a radically different approach to the sexual body, in much the same way that I find pleasure in Warhol's films. As Judith Mayne notes, "one could hardly find a contemporary woman's film more saturated with authorial signature than *je tu il elle*". It is perhaps the difficulty of the avant-garde re-representation of the female body that makes this film so memorable. The fact that the main woman character is played by the film-maker herself tends to move the critic into a discussion of subjectivity beyond the realm of the film frame.

(From: *Identity and Memory: The Films of Chantal Akerman*, Gwendolyn Audrey Foster, Flicks Books, Wiltshire, 1999: 2. With thanks to Gwendolyn Audrey Foster and to Matt Stevens at Flicks Books for permission to reprint this text.)

MISCELLANEOUS

A note about versions

La Chambre is sometimes called *La Chambre 2* – which we presume refers to the fact that the selected take was take 2.

La Chambre is generally shown mute. However, Babette Mangolte confirmed for us that Akerman had once experimented with sound, using the following text as a basis. The retrospective played the film mute, because Akerman told us that this was what she would prefer.

Babette Mangolte says that the second act of *je tu il elle*, the truck driver episode, was shot in 16mm and blown up to match the rest which was shot on 35mm. Prints were made on 35mm stock.

Text of Adam Roberts' introductory remarks

La Chambre – which is to say: the room, or chamber even…

A so-so print – but a print that shows itself – the very stuff of it – with some dirt and scratches. We've kept the sound head open so you can hear the print, hear its history.

And there is Akerman herself – not as protagonist, as she was in *L'Enfant aimé*, but now looking at us – fidgeting – perhaps a little impatiently?

This is a film that nods to Michael Snow of course, but Akerman's being present, there onscreen, announces a very different sort of project – she is asking us to rethink how we look… not as in a Warhol Screen Test where the subject often fidgets under the scrutiny, but in another way, that invites us who look at the film, into the moment. We can't help but become aware…

After *La Chambre*, we have *Le 15/8* – made in Paris – yet harking back to New York that Akerman had got to know in the 1970s – the worlds of Anthology Film Archives and of Judson Church and lofts on the Lower East Side – where she soaked up the modernist fever and made films informed by all of that – *Hotel Monterey* and *La Chambre* especially…

…. but Akerman for *Le 15/8* was back in Europe where the figure of the woman is framed by the legacy of centuries of fine art representation…

I think that's not unimportant–- because the 15th of August is the Feast of the Assumption – when Mary, Mother of God was bodily assumed into Heaven… transformed from flesh into art, or from denigrated state into idealised state… I wonder if you will find that a useful point of view?

A detail that caught my eye in *Le 15/8* is how actor Chris Myllykoski's hand hovers. I was reminded of the debate about the raised hand of the actor figure in Beckett's *Ghost Trio* – something about the idea of marionette, of the Romantic era's dread of automatism…

Because that's what I found myself thinking about how Akerman shows us film as a kind of reinvention of cinema – the locked-off shot, the duration, the solidity, the audibility of things and men and women – particularly women – as she makes us see them… to me as exciting as, say, Buster Keaton's films.

To go back to Beckett – he referred to Kleist's essay on marionettes: which made a case for the marionette as sublime, transcending not only the limits and flaws of the human body, but also the weight of self-consciousness. Self-awareness, he maintained, bred affectation, which destroys natural grace and charm in man. "Man is, therefore, a creature permanently off balance. He lacks the unity, harmony, symmetry and grace that characterises the puppet".

We'll have a short break before *je tu il elle* – which should be a shock and wonderful revelation to you if you haven't seen it – or you will have seen it before and won't need to hear anything from us at all…

La Chambre text

Reproduced with the kind permission of Sylviane Akerman and La Fondation Akerman. The author of the translation is unknown.

Tu m'as tiré les cheveux et tu as disparu avant même que j'ai pu te battre ou crier alors je suis restée immobile et me suis détournée, j'ai redescendu les escaliers glissants et je me suis retrouvée dehors, l'aéroport était blanc de soleil, j'ai marché tout droit, un moment je me suis arrêtée pour demander le bus, et j'ai continué à marcher, j'ai pris le bus sans presque le savoir, je me suis endormie, je me suis réveillée, je suis descendue du bus à Grand Central – j'ai pris la 42ème rue, j'ai regardé trois fois une montre et je suis sûre qu'elle retardait d'une heure alors seulement j'ai commencé à courir jusqu'au métro. Je t'écris que je pleurais en courant, le soleil surexposait la ruelle, j'ai pris l'IND. Dans le train un gros noir ouvrait la bouche dans un sourire-grimace et la fermait pour recommencer à l'ouvrir.

Il n'y avait que lui et moi dans le train, je suis descendue très loin de la maison et j'ai marché, je suis montée lentement et je me suis jetée sur le lit, je me suis relevée pour vérifier les deux horloges, elles marquaient la même heure 10h30, elles devaient sans doute retarder d'une heure. Je me suis recouchée, j'ai dormi sur le ventre, la tête dans les bras, je ne pouvais pas voir si tu n'étais pas là. J'ai dormi jusqu'à minuit, sans doute une heure, je me suis levée, j'ai sorti tous les vêtements de l'armoire, pris tout ceux qui étaient sales d'un côté, tout ceux qui étaient à coudre de l'autre et rejeté les propres dans l'armoire, j'ai fait l'ourlet du pantalon rose assise par terre sur le tapis près du lit la […] entre mes jambes, j'ai tout laissé par terre je me suis recouchée, j'ai vu que le lit était plein de sang, je me suis relevée j'ai fermé toutes les lumières sauf celle de la cuisine, je me suis recouchée sur le ventre et j'ai commencé à me masturber violement je me suis dit que maintenant j'aurais tout l'espace que je voulais, l'envie m'a passé aussitôt, j'ai retiré ma main de mon sexe et je me suis couchée sur le dos et j'ai commencé à t'écrire dans ma tête alors je me suis relevée il était 3h donc 4h et j'ai commencé à t'écrire sur la table de cuisine entre le […] et l'ananas. Je t'embrasse très fort. Chantal.

You pulled my hair and disappeared even before I could hit you or cry out loud. So I lay quite still and turned away. I headed back down the slippery stairs and found myself outside. The sun and the airport ahead. I walked down the street for a while, paused to hail a bus. I walked some more, took a bus without thinking. I fell asleep, woke and got off the bus at Grand Central. I headed along 42nd Street. I looked at my watch three times to be sure it was only an hour later. I ran to the subway. I'm writing to you to say that I cried as I ran, the blinding sun in my eyes. I took the IND. On the train a big black man opened his mouth, to reveal a smile, or maybe a grimace. He shut his mouth only to open it again. It was just him and me on the

train, so I got off miles from home and walked. I climbed slowly
to my bed and threw myself down. I got up to check the time on
two clocks, both showed it was 10:30. Presumably both running
an hour behind. I went back to bed, fell asleep on my stomach,
with my head in my arms. I could not tell if you were there or
not. I slept a while, maybe for an hour. I got up, emptied all
wardrobe of clothes, and divided them into those that were
dirty, those that need mending, and the rest that I tossed back
clean into the wardrobe. I hemmed the pink pants sitting on the
rug on the floor, by the bed. I left everything that was between
my legs on the floor. I turned round and noticed that the bed
was covered in blood. I got up to switch off all the lights except
the one in the kitchen. I lay back down on my stomach and I
began to wank off roughly. I told myself: now I have all the space
I want. The urge died suddenly. I took my hand off my sex and
lay on my back. I started to write to you in my head. I got up. It
was 3, then 4. I started writing to you, sitting at the kitchen table
between the [...] and the pineapple. Hugs. Chantal.

Akerman 3

JEANNE DIELMAN, 23 QUAI DU COMMERCE, 1080 BRUXELLES

BILLING

A Nos Amours continues a retrospective of the complete film
works of Chantal Akerman, with her celebrated second feature
film *Jeanne Dielman, 23 Quai du Commerce, 1080 Bruxelles*.
An astonishing, crystalline film that is as arresting and absorbing
as it ever was. A tour de force: assured, confident, awe-inspiring.
A landmark of cinema.

Chantal Akerman is a film-maker whose time has come: it is
news that stays news. It is a cinema that reinvents and redefines
what film is and can do. Akerman's work is superficially wide-
ranging – documentary and narrative, film and video, 16mm and
35mm, cinema and gallery – and yet her work is characterised
by an uncompromising and singular sense of purpose. What
Akerman shows us, by means structural and otherwise, is
nothing less than the human condition, a series of astonishing
mediations on loneliness and anxiety, alienation and discomfort.
Akerman so quickly, from her earliest work, established a
startling and provocative project that is among the very greatest
in European film.

As J Hoberman has said: 'Comparable in force and originality
to Godard or Fassbinder, Chantal Akerman is arguably the most
important European director of her generation'.

Film theorist Laura Mulvey will introduce the screening.

***Jeanne Dielman, 23 Quai du Commerce,
1080 Bruxelles*** (1975, 201')

Preparing to see *Jeanne Dielman*...

ICA Bulletin, 10 December 2013, see page 179.

THE HAND-OUT

Akerman 3: *Jeanne Dielman, 23 Quai du Commerce, 1080 Bruxelles*

Thursday 12 December 2013. ICA Cinema, 7pm. introduced by Laura Mulvey.

Jeanne Dielman, 23 Quai du Commerce, 1080 Bruxelles

With: Delphine Seyrig, Jan Decorte, Henri Storck, Jacques Doniol-Valcroze, Yves Bical; Assistant directors: Marilyn Watelet, Serge Brodsky, Marianne de Muylder; Cinematography: Babette Mangolte; Camera operator: Dominique Delesalle; Script supervisors: Danae Maroulacou, Bernie Deswarte, Françoise Van Thienen; Art direction: Philippe Graff; Editing: Patricia Canino; Location sound: Bénie Deswarte, Françoise Van Thienen; Sound editor: Alain Marchal; Foley: Jacky Dufour; Re-recording mixer: Jean-Paul Loublier; Production: Evelyn Paul, Corinne Jénart; 1975 35mm colour 201'.

Chantal Akerman: I do think it's a feminist film because I give space to things which were never, almost never, shown in that way, like the daily gestures of a woman. They are in the lowest hierarchy of film images. A kiss or a car crash come higher, and I don't think that's an accident. It's because these are women's gestures that they count for so little. That's one reason I think it's a feminist film.

But more than content, it's because of the style. If you choose to show a woman's gestures so precisely, it's because you love them. In some way you recognise those gestures that have always been denied and ignored. I think that the real problem with women's films usually has nothing to do with the content. It's that hardly any women really have the confidence enough to carry through on their feelings. Instead the content is the most simple and obvious thing. They deal with that and forget to look for formal ways to express what they are and what they want, their own rhythms, their own way of looking at things. A lot of women have unconscious contempt for their feelings. But I don't think I do. I have enough confidence in myself. So that's the other reason why I think it's a feminist film – not just what it says but what is shown and how it's shown....

I didn't have any doubts about any of the shots. I was very sure of where to put the camera and when and why. It's the first time I had that feeling so strongly....

You know who is looking; you always know what the point of view is, all the time. It's always the same. But still, I was looking with a great deal of attention and the attention wasn't distanced. It was not a neutral look – that doesn't exist anyhow. For me, the way I looked at what was going on was a look of love and respect. Maybe that's difficult to understand but I really think that's it. I let her live her life in the middle of the frame. I didn't go in too close, but was not very far away. I let her be in her space. It's not uncontrolled. But the camera was not voyeuristic in the commercial way because you always knew where I was. You know, it wasn't shot through the keyhole....

It was the only way to shoot that scene and shoot that film – to avoid cutting women into a hundred pieces, to avoid cutting the action in a hundred places, to look carefully and to be respectful. The framing was meant to respect the space, her, and her gestures within it....

We didn't have a lot of choice about where to put the camera because I didn't want angle shots. I wanted them all to be straight, as much as possible....

Delphine said, "Why do you use such a low angle?" I said, "No, I didn't want to do that. That's not how I see the world." It was never shot from the point of view of the son or anyone else. It's always me. Because the other way is manipulation. The son is not the camera; the son is her son. If the son looks at the mother, it's because you asked him to do it. So you

should look at the son looking at the mother, and not have
the camera in place of the son looking at the mother...

It's really a hard problem to try to say what differentiates
a woman's rhythm in film because a man can use the same
forms of expression. I don't know if we have the words, if they
exist yet. I don't think we know enough about women's film
even to... I can talk about myself but I can't speak in a general,
theoretical way at all. I just think that I've finally reached that
point meaning that I agree with what I do. It's not like I feel
one way and my work expresses something else. But I can't
define it any more theoretically. We speak of 'women's rhythm',
but it isn't necessarily the same for all women. I also think
that Hollywood doesn't express a man's rhythm either, but the
rhythm of capitalism or fascism. Men are cheated by it, too.

But you know, some theorists say it is because we experience
pleasure in another way than men do. Sexual pleasure. I really
think that in movies it's right there. When I saw *Hotel Monterey*
this morning, I really thought it was an erotic film. I felt that way
– la jouissance du voir.

(From *Chantal Akerman on* Jeanne Dielman, *Camera Obscura* (1977) Fall vol 1,
no 2: 118. With thanks to Diane Grosse and Duke University Press for permission
to reprint.)

Akerman 4

NEWS FROM HOME

BILLING

*A Nos Amour*s continues a retrospective of the complete
film works of Chantal Akerman with *News from home*
(1976), a film that engages with her mother, with absence
and displacement.

Akerman arrived in New York in 1976, having blazed a trail in
Europe with her extraordinary *Jeanne Dielman*. She was travelling
with letters her mother had written to her during her previous
extended stay in the city – in 1972 – when she had encountered
and so profoundly engaged with the avant garde scene, in
particular with the work of Michael Snow , and shot her own
Hotel Monterey and *La Chambre*. These letters would provide
the soundtrack for a new film (*News from home*): accounts of
daily life, life as lived in distant Belgium, invoked by means of
observation and snippets of news. These are thoughts and feelings
shared in letter form by a mother with her very distant daughter.

Image-wise, the new film would show New York, its streets,
subways, denizens. There are city streets framed by tall
buildings, subways and diners, with some tracking, but not
much. The citizens going about their business take notice or
not. Sounds might be in synch or not. This is not a smart city: it
is a city of ghettos and decline.

Mother and daughter comment and conjoin: 'I live to the rhythm
of your letters', or, 'you always write the same thing and I have the
impression you don't say anything'. Who is addressing whom is no
simple matter. Absence and displacement are the invariable themes.

Akerman has described her murmuring voiceover as psalmody
(the singing of psalms or similar sacred canticles, especially in

public worship), which perfectly evokes the prayerful effect, the mingling of longing, the provoking of guilt, and the offer of love. The closing scenes, scenes of departure and voyage, play without the presence of the voice, without complex maternal comfort. Such an absence allows perhaps for a new note of optimism – to proceed one must depart.

'This is one of the best depictions of the alienation of exile that I know' *Jonathan Rosenbaum.*

A Nos Amours will screen the restored DCP English-language version, and after an interval, a 16mm print of the original French-language version, both voiced by Akerman.

Introduced by novelist and film-maker Xiaolu Guo.

News From Home (2 x 89')

BLOG
Planning a screening: *News from home*
ICA Bulletin, 21 January 2014, see page 183.

THE HAND-OUT
Akerman 4: *News from home*
Thursday 23 January 2014. ICA Cinema, 7pm. Introduced by novelist and film-maker Xiaolu Guo.

News from home
Letters written by Natalia Akerman; Reader of the letters: Chantal Akerman; Camera: Babette Mangolte and Jim Asbell; Editing: Francine Sandberg; Sound: Dominique Dalmasso and Larry Haas; 1976 16mm colour 89'; French- and English-language versions.

A Nos Amours will screen the digitised English-language version (DCP), and after a 10-minute interval, a 16mm print of the French-language version (without subtitles), both voiced by Akerman.

Raymond Bellour: There is no photograph(y) in *News from home*, but there is the photographic. This means that most of the shots are like fixed and often very long photographic exposures in which movement may take place, but it is a kind of uncertain, open, documentary movement, something like the development of what a snapshot captures. The rare camera movements are pans that sweep the surface without entering the real body of the city, New York, where the heroine/auteur of the film lives, far from her native Belgium. We could, for example, make a comparison with the famous forward tracking shots of Resnais in *Hiroshima mon amour* (1959) to underline what a genuinely cinematographic incarnation of a city (or rather two: Nevers, Hiroshima) might resemble, as opposed to what in Chantal Akerman's film becomes its photographic capturing. But that's already considering it in an old-fashioned way, out of a need to establish distinctions: her film is no less a film than is Resnais'. Quite simply, it is a moment of cinema captured from now on by photography.

This impression grows stronger because we do not see the auteur but only her eye, which we assume is identified with this camera that sits and waits, with a marvellous sense of framing and of time, for something real to happen – even if it must wait a long time, and in the dull indifference broken by sudden jolts that is so specific to photographic activity. There is, for example, an extraordinary, very long shot, in the subway: on the platform, five pillars that are irregularly laid out delimit three terrace-like spaces for the two train tracks, the double platform that separates them (unlike the layout of the Paris métro), and the two platforms bordering them on both sides. The strength of the spatial dimension of the shot is directly related to the fact that everything seems flat, as if squashed onto a single level, despite the levels of depth one can make out: these levels only come back to life during events (people walking around, trains coming into the station), before evaporating again. To such an extent that this interminable shot looks like a series of prolonged snapshots, interrupted by brief moments when life returns.

The impression of photography comes from the very subject of the film, its principle: a mother, in Brussels, diligently sends banal letters to her daughter who has left the family home to try to live and work in New York. The daughter reads the mother's letters, in a sing-song, monotonous, and detached voice, these letters in which the mother gently complains that her daughter writes so little. She also demands photographs, naturally, and this again emphasises the photographic effect of the letter, this conversation immobilised in time, this sort of "freeze-text".

Between the image and the text, therefore, a strange frozen circulation sets in. A division. On the one hand, there is the capturing, fragmented, silent, elliptic gaze of the daughter—an eye in its natural state, so to speak — that strives to observe itself while discovering the city; on the other, there is her voice. One gets the feeling that she only reveals her absent mother's words in this way in order to give them over more effectively, via a kind of calculated sadism, to their undivided solitude.

(Originally published in Raymond Bellour, *Between-the-Images*, *Documents* series, translated by Allyn Hardyck, JRP|Ringier and les presses du réel, Zurich and Dijon 2012, p. 164. Thanks to Raymond Bellour and Clément Dirié for permission to reprint.)

MISCELLANEOUS

News from home – **transcript of English-language version**
Dear child. I received your letter and hope you will write often. I hope you won't stay away too long and that you've found a job by now. If you're doing well, we're happy. Even though we do miss you. When will you be back? Everything is fine here, but Sylviane is home with the flu. My blood pressure is low. I'm on medication for it. Today is my birthday. I feel sad. It's quiet at the shop. Tonight we're going out to dinner with friends. That's all. Your birthday is coming up. I wish you all the best. Write to me soon about your work, about New York, about everything. Lots of love from the three of us. Your loving mother.

My dear girl. I'm so glad you wrote back so soon. Your letter made me feel much better. I'm happy you're doing better. Father enjoys it when I read your letters to him. We're not angry that you left so suddenly, but keep us up to speed now. I dream about you a lot and your letters really cheer me up. Father and I work hard. The winter season is over. Summer is coming. The weather is mild, I hope it stays that way. My health isn't very good. I often feel hot and weak. I thought it was just my age, but it's not. So I'm back on my medication. Sylviane had the flu. She has gone back to school now. Father has to lose four kilos. He's on a diet and takes medicine. Other than that, everything's fine. Sweetheart, we hope that everything will work out the way you want it. Lots of love from Daddy, Sylviane and the rest. Your loving mother.

Dear Chantal. I sent you some summer clothes, because it must be warm there. I hope I have the right address. I didn't receive a letter this week. Last week three letters and this week none. I hope you did receive my letters. But sometimes it says New York 10025 on your envelope, other times 10027. Which one is it? This summer, we are going to spend some weekends at sea instead of going abroad. I hope the shop will pick up a little. We have already started with the winter collection. The son of one of my nieces is studying medicine. Why don't you go see his parents in the Bronx? They know you want to make films. I hope you write back soon. Lots of love from Daddy, Sylviane and the rest. Your loving mother. I sent some summer clothes to your last address. Why did you move? I hope you get the parcel soon. I already paid for the postage. I hope you won't have to pay anything. If you need money, I can send you some dollars. I hope the heat isn't bothering you too much over there. Just buy a pair of good sandals. I'm sure you can find them there. I hope you get through the summer all right. I'm only receiving one letter a week. Please try and write more often. Your letters cheer

me up. We're proud that you're doing well. Be careful when
you go out on the street at night. New York is dangerous. We're
going to Knokke for a few days. I'm feeling very tired again. I'm
going to have another massage. Sylviane is taking her exams.
Dearest, your father and I send you big kisses. Please write soon.
Your loving mother. And write to Aunt Tonia some time.

Dearest. I got your letter. I was worried because I hadn't heard
anything for two weeks. Did you receive the summer clothes?
Please let me know soon. I haven't heard from Colette, but I'll
send you some dollars now and then. What kind of work are you
doing at that restaurant? I'm glad you're learning English. That
will come in handy. Even so, I miss you and hope to see you soon.
Sylviane misses you, too. At night she sometimes dreams you're
back. Tonight we're going to visit some friends. Everyone is tired.
Danny said to say hi. We ran into him at a dance. It's too bad that
She's feeling down. Jean-Pierre found someone else and wants a
divorce. She's at a loss what to do. Dearest, please write often and
let me know whether you got the parcel. Lots of love and see you
soon. From Father, Sylviane and Mother and the rest of the family
who often asks about you. Your loving mother.

Dearest, I got your last letter ten days ago. I'm wondering
what happened. I sent you twenty dollars. Let us hear from
you soon. You know how important your letters are to me.
Tonia is also curious to know how you're doing. Why don't you
write to her? We don't have much news. The summer wasn't
very special. But the next days will be very hot. The business
is quiet. Father is worried and I get bored a lot in the store.
Sylviane finished her exams and she often keeps me company
now. We don't do much in the evenings. We watch TV a lot.
Dearest, we think of you a lot and hope you're doing well.
Don't forget about us. Kisses from Daddy, Sylviane and your
loving mother.

Dearest. I got your letter soon after I had written to you.
I'm glad everything is going well. But do write a little more
often. You're busy, but try and write some more anyway. I
understand you won't be coming back for now. I miss you a
lot. We celebrated Judith's birthday. I'll send you some photos.
Her speech is improving and she's starting to read. She's a real
beauty. Right away she jumped on Daddy's lap. Why did Lilly
want to have a baby so soon? It's hard on both of them. On July
18 we celebrated Sylviane's birthday. Without you. I'm sorry, the
most important thing is for you to be happy. Lots of love from
me and from Daddy who misses you, too. Your loving mother
who thinks about you often.

Dear child of mine. I'm glad you don't have that job anymore and
that you're liking New York so much. People around here don't
understand it. They think New York is terrible. But perhaps they
were too quick to judge. I hope your new flat is affordable and
isn't in a dangerous area. What do you do for a living? Yesterday
we went to Sonia. We had a good time. We met new people whom
we invited to our house this Thursday. Father has been very tired
lately. He's been sleeping poorly and wakes often. He has many
worries. That's why the distraction is good. I'm doing better, but
there's always something. Sylviane is really growing up. It's too
bad she can be a bit apathetic. I hope she doesn't turn out like
my sister. We are having a heatwave. I hope it won't last long. I'm
sending you a photo of Judith's birthday. Never mind the way I
look. Why don't you send us a photo? Lots of love from all of us.
Big kisses and see you soon. Your loving mother.

Dearest girl. I wish I could finally give you a big hug again.
Judith wrote to you. She's hoping you'll write back. Once again:
did you receive the 20 dollars I sent you a month ago? Please
answer my questions for once. For Heaven's sake. Please try.
How are you doing? Where and with whom are you living? How

much are you paying? Do me a favour and go and see your uncle once in a while. Eric and Chris had a little girl. They are overjoyed. They have to find a bigger house. Chris has gotten a taste for it, she says. Nothing much is happening here. Too bad you're missing Sylviane's birthday. But as long as you're happy in New York, that's what's most important. I don't expect to see you back anytime soon. Should you need anything, just let me know. I talked to Marilyn the other day. She no longer likes her job. It may be silly, this way she risks being fired, but it's up to her. Just let me know what you want me to send with her. Please write again soon. That's the important thing. Father is always very happy when we get another letter from you. Everyone is asking about you. Darling, lots of love from me, Daddy, Sylviane and the rest of the family. Your mommy sends you a kiss.

My darling daughter. I'm sorry I took a while to write back. I received your screenplay. I think it's written very well. Those people sure have a hard life. You really did a good job. I hope you'll be able to shake up public opinion about these social evils. I'm enclosing 20 dollars, I don't dare send more. I'll send some with Marilyn. Father had a dream about you last night. You were back and then you were gone. He was sad all day. I wasn't sure how to help him. Write soon. When he knows you're doing well, his fears go away. Sweetheart, if only you knew how proud your father is of you. If I had the money, I'd come and see you, but I'd have to win the lottery first. Everything is fine here. We're working hard. Father is far too kind. A customer who still owed us money, went broke. So goodbye, money. As long as one has their health, that's the main thing. I hope business will pick up this season. Father took out a credit insurance that will cover 80 per cent. This kind of misfortune happens more and more. I won't trouble you with it anymore. We just won't give up hope. Father is looking for a patch of land to build a house on. It's his big dream. We will have to sell the flat and take out an extra mortgage. I would love it, a house with a little garden. Sweetheart, write as often as possible. We want to know how you're doing. It's great that you're doing so well. Lots of love from the three of us. We hope you'll write soon. I received your letter and am happy you received the 20 dollars. I also sent a cheque for 100 dollars to your new address. I hope you received that as well. Marilyn isn't leaving yet. That has to do with Michel's work if necessary, I'll send you some more money. I'm glad you're doing well. Your letter has reassured me. I hope you're managing financially. I'll send some more money. I just hope the letter doesn't get lost. Perhaps I can send some with Colette. We are closing the store in Tournai. It was hard work and didn't bring in much. I hope the sale will bring in a little extra. I haven't been feeling well at all. I always feel listless in the summer. Perhaps I will take a break for a few days during the vacation. Lilia thanks you for your letter. Did you write to Sonia and Ida? Lots of love from Daddy, Sylviane and the rest of the family. Write soon, sweetheart. Your loving mother.

Dear daughter. Thank you for your letter. I'm glad you received the money at your new address. Father was at home sick. He had a throat abscess and high fever. I took care of him myself. Luckily the abscess burst yesterday. Thankfully he feels better now. Without him the office is a mess. I'm very tired now. I look awful. Eline will be married on August 25. I'm not going, I'll send a telegram. How are you doing? I've been worried about you. I wish you could just be home with us. Take care, sweetheart. I'm enclosing another 20 dollars. Daddy is still too weak to write, but he sends you lots of love. Big kisses from all of us. Your loving mother.

My dear daughter. Thank you for your letter. I'm just sorry it was such a short note. I know you're busy, but do try and write to us.

I want to know how you're doing and if you're in good health.
Everything is fine over here. Father's throat is getting better.
We've been working hard again at the store. But it's not easy.
I usually don't start until noon. Danny passed his exams. He's
going to study photography in Paris. His parents have accepted
it, although they would have preferred something else. I haven't
seen them since their vacation in Spain. They did call: it was
hot and crowded and they're never going back again. Everyone
is asking about you. Lots of love from Daddy, Sylviane and the
family. Your loving mother.

My dear daughter. I'm sorry I didn't write back immediately.
Marilyn told me she won't be going to New York anytime soon.
She sounded sad, but said that everything was going well. You
mentioned a different job. I hope it's interesting and not too
tiresome. I hope you're managing financially, for I can't send
anything this month. You haven't mentioned your uncle. Go
see him. He's family, after all. Irvine's daughter Alice is getting
engaged. Guess to whom. To Gilbert. He isn't handsome, but
he is sweet. Alice loves him. Gilbert's parents already bought
an apartment. Next month we're going to the engagement
party. Sweetheart, we haven't seen each other in a long time.
Daddy misses you a lot and hopes you're taking good care of
yourself. If you think you should stay longer, we will accept it.
I don't have much news. Aunt Nadia isn't feeling too well. She
thinks it's something gynaecological. She'll be examined soon.
Hopefully it's nothing serious. Sweetheart, lots of love from us.
Daddy hopes to see you soon again. Your loving mother who is
thinking of you.

My dear girl. I'm so glad you had such good news and wrote to
us right away. But you didn't say whether you were planning
to stay in New York. I miss you tremendously. But even though
you'll be staying longer, I'm not sad. The main thing is that

you're happy. When will you send us some photos? Lily and Alain are fighting. When they see each other, they ignore each other. It's definitely over, she says. Alain isn't right for her. She will be writing you soon. She sends her regards. I have another toothache. They're going to pull two molars in September. Other than that, everything's fine. The shop is doing better. The customers are very enthusiastic. Daddy is right: work is good for a person. Etty was here on Sunday with Daphna. What a nice, smart girl she is. The trousers you sent her look good on her. Darling, write soon and send some photos. Love from all of us. Your loving mother.

Dear girl. I had to wait a long time for another letter. Please try to write more often. Furthermore, I was alone. Daddy went to Italy and Sylviane was out of town. How are you doing? You mentioned you had a new job. What does it entail? I'm glad you have so many friends. Everything is fine here. Daddy's trip to Italy was hectic, but useful. Sunday we visited with the aunts. It was very nice. Aunt Nadia isn't ill anymore. Father had a good time, too. You were the only one missing. Father found some land for the house. He wants to build a separate floor for you, where you can live quietly soon. I'm a bit worried about the extra mortgage, but I try not to show it. I hope everything will be all right. Sweetheart, write soon. Lots of love from Daddy, Sylviane and the family. Your loving mother.

My dear girl. I'm responding to your letter right away. I'm glad you're managing. Eric called me right away when he got back from New York. He told me about where you live, that you looked good but he didn't say anything about your return. Do you still have the same job? You must be speaking English very well by now. During the strike I was staying by the sea. It made me feel better. Many of our friends were there. Other than that, nothing special. Sweetheart, lots of love from Daddy, Sylviane and the rest. Write back soon, darling. Your loving mother.

My darling girl. I was starting to get worried when I got a letter from you indirectly. I will send something for you. Something small, because I don't have much time. Now and then I have the feeling I'm suffocating in the store. But on other days I enjoy it. Don't be angry when I ask you again when you're coming back. If I hear from you regularly, I don't get so worried. So write more often. You never write how you're really doing. How is your job? Do you have friends there? Father thinks you're lonely. We went to the engagement party. We danced until three o'clock. It has cheered up your father. Freddy is in the hospital with thrombosis. He's in a bad state. But I think he will make it. It won't be long though, before he won't have anyone to take care of him. Lily and Alain have definitely broken up. I hope you'll write again soon. Sweetheart, lots of love from all of us.

My dear girl. Finally a sign of life from you after two weeks of silence. But I'm happy with the letter and the photos. You look great in them. Father thought so, too. You look pretty with long hair. I miss you even more now. It's terribly quiet over here. Father started his vacation already and comes with me to the shop now. That's always better than sitting at home. I'm still tired, despite a number of injections. I'm not complaining. Next week we're going to spend some days by the sea. School will be starting again soon. Sylviane is ready to go. That was all, darling. Please write a bit about your work and your life there. My dear girl. Last night we were pleasantly surprised to find your letter. I read it to Father right away. It made our day. It's been raining here for days. I'm feeling very listless. Every morning I get up feeling tired. At night I feel better. Father wants me to change my GP. Sylviane has been very helpful. On Sunday we visited with Judith and Simon...

Akerman 5

BILLING

A Nos Amours continues a retrospective of the complete film works of Chantal Akerman with *Les Rendez-vous d'Anna* (1978), a polished, forlorn fable of isolation.

Anna Silver is a film-maker. Her mother and sick father live in Belgium. Her frequent travels mean that hotel rooms are home as much as anywhere. Visits to the parental home are fleeting affairs – confessional intimacies between mother and daughter must be taken wherever they can. Pickups are easy-come-easy-go affairs. Commitment is provisional. 'Anna, where are you?' a voice enquires. Anna may not know or much care.

The reflexive, seemingly autobiographical nature of all these components needs no underlining, and this hall-of-mirrors effect can be superficially disorientating. But a true bearing is sustained by the luminous, painterly miracle of wonderful image-making, and the sure sense of a great mind at work, exploring the alienating topographies of contemporary Europe.

Here is dislocation amid the faux-comforts of hotels, endless peregrinations according to inescapably rigorous train timetables, nomadism as a form of deferred existential crisis. And a growing, nagging suspicion that for Akerman, indeed for any sensitive being, the spectre of the Nazis' Final Solution haunts the trains and soulless places of Europe.

A profound work of art that finds Akerman exploring a new, seemingly Bressonian idiom, that plumbs the well's depth.

Chris Petit will introduce this screening of *Les Rendez-vous d'Anna*. Chris Petit is a film-maker whose concern with journeys, flux and the transitory has been so marked from his debut feature *Radio On* to his recent London Orbital.

BLOG

On Chantal Akerman's *Les Rendez-vous d'Anna*

ICA Bulletin, 12 February 2014, see page 186.

THE HAND-OUT

Akerman 5: *Les Rendez-vous d'Anna*

Thursday 13 February 2014. ICA Cinema, 7.30pm.

Les Rendez-vous d'Anna

Introduced by film-maker Chris Petit; With: Aurore Clément, Helmut Griem, Magali Noël, Hanns Zischler, Lea Massari Jean-Pierre Cassel, Alain Berenboom.Assistant directors: Romain Goupil, Marilyn Watelet; Cinematography: Jean Penzer; Camera operator: Michel Houssiau; Sound recording: Henri Morelle; Production design: Philippe Graff; Art direction: Andre Fonteyne; Editing: Francine Sandberg; Sound editor: Suzanne Sandberg; Rerecording mixer: Jean-Paul Loublier; Producer: Alain Dahan; 1978 35mm colour 127'. French with English subtitles.

Michael Koresky: In the years between *je tu il elle* and her fourth feature, *Les Rendez-vous d'Anna* (1978), Chantal Akerman had become an art-film sensation, thanks to *Jeanne Dielman, 23 Quai du Commerce, 1080 Bruxelles*. Her ultimate expression of the reassurance and anxiety of routine and her most evocative visual exploration of space and time, *Jeanne Dielman* tied Akerman's distinct long-duration camera approach to a challengingly drawn-out narrative of domestic confinement. Made with an entirely female crew and focusing on the stultifying household routines of an isolated woman, it was hailed in Europe and America as possibly the greatest, purest feminist film ever made, even if Akerman insisted that was not her intention.

With such adulation came hefty expectations for her next narrative feature, and though *Les Rendez-vous d'Anna* clearly had much in common with *Jeanne Dielman* (aesthetic spareness and impeccable structural integrity, as well as the use of a major leading actress), the film was considered a failure. One of the reasons for this was its rejection, on political grounds, by many of those who had embraced *Jeanne Dielman*, since Anna was funded by a major, male-owned film company (Gaumont) and Akerman was working with a crew composed mostly of men, among them, for the first time, cinematographer Jean Penzer (*The Two of Us*).

"All the women who went to see *Jeanne Dielman* . . . didn't want to see *Les rendez-vous d'Anna*, because they said I was already corrupted," Akerman later said. "Can you imagine that?" Yet what this controversy proved, especially to those who may not have seen her pre-*Jeanne Dielman* work, was that Akerman's films were not agenda-driven. The elegant, odd beauty of *Les Rendez-vous d'Anna* is its refusal to fit into any generic or political parameters; like its wandering protagonist, it's unattached and searching.

The film can't help but come across as autobiographical, since its heroine, played by Aurore Clément (*Lacombe, Lucien*), is a Belgian film-maker. Like all of Akerman's main characters to this point (*je tu il elle*'s Julie; *News from home*'s unseen letter recipient; *Jeanne Dielman*), Anna does not express her feelings through dialogue but through action or non-action, or by simply listening to others – her reserve is a protective shell against an alien world. Akerman further represents this estrangement by situating Anna in stark environments: she is travelling through Northern Europe on a tour to promote her latest film, and Akerman shoots every city and town she visits as if it were the same arid nowheresville. Through Anna's meetings, whether with a one-night stand (Helmut Griem), an ex-lover (Jean-Pierre Cassel), or her mother (Lea Massari), we begin to piece together the details of her life and her profound disconnection from everyone and everything. *Les Rendez-vous d'Anna* is a film about a voyage, though the destination and purpose are unclear. And as with many of Akerman's films, before and since, it's also a story of displacement. Like the attractive stranger (Hanns Zischler) Anna meets on the train to Brussels, who's lived in six different countries, Akerman has been constantly on the move since the 70s, making films not only in New York and all over Europe, but also in Tel Aviv, Texas and Mexico. She's director as nomad.

(Originally published in 2010 for the Criterion Collection's release *Eclipse Series 19: Chantal Akerman in the Seventies*. Thanks to Michael Koresky, Anna Thorngate and Criterion for permission to reprint.)

Akerman 6

BILLING

A Nos Amours continues a retrospective of the complete film works of Chantal Akerman with *Dis-moi* (1980) in which the film-maker, herself a daughter of a Holocaust survivor, engages for the first time with the Shoah.

Dis-moi was commissioned for television – part of a series about grandmothers (*Grands-mères, un série proposée par Jean Frapat*). Akerman chose to talk with several elderly Jewish women – all of them survivors of the Shoah. Akerman has a terrible family history of her own – 'My mother arrived in Brussels in 1938 from a small town near Krakow. In 1942 she was taken to Auschwitz, just 30 miles from where she grew up… Her parents died there and most of her family' (from an interview in *The Jewish Chronicle*). Akerman's mother Natalia, a teenager at the time, survived, a quite unimaginable orphaning.

The film-maker is in the frame and conducts the interviews, bearing witness to stories told by these elderly but dignified women survivors. But there is comedy here, too – after all, these are stubborn, tough and wayward women who if bored are quite capable of losing interest in interviews and film crews, preferring to switch on the TV. Nothing invokes the European disaster better than these encounters with orphans of the Shoah – cut off from the past and themselves by the experience of horror.

Subtitled in English for the first time by *A Nos Amour*s, translated by Sylvie Beaufils.

Screening with *Autour de Jeanne Dielman*, Sami Frey's documentary video shot on the set of *Jeanne Dielman*, edited by Chantal Akerman and Agnès Ravez.

BLOG

BLOG

***Dis-moi:* a breakthrough work by Chantal Akerman.**

HuffPo, 4 March 2014. See page 188.

THE HAND-OUT

Akerman 6*: Dis-moi & Autour de Jeanne Dielman*

Thursday 13 March 2014. ICA Cinema, 8pm.

Dis-moi

(aka *Aujourd'hui, dis-moi*); Camera: Maurice Perrimond, Michel Davaud, Francis Lapeyre; Sound: Xavier Vauthrin. André Siekierski; Editing: Francine Sandberg; Sound mix: Elvire Lerner; Produced by Michèle Boig; 1980 16mm transferred to video colour 6'; French, with English subtitles, cued live by Charlotte Maconochie. Translated by Sylvie Beaufils, Charlotte Maconochie, and as below.

Akerman was asked by French Television (TF1) to make a film about grandmothers. She chose to interview her mother (an audio interview only), and then film a series of elderly Jewish women – all Holocaust survivors – talking about their lives and experiences.

Interviewees sang and remembered songs from the lost world of the Polish shtetls where they grew up. Given the Holocaust, the dialects used could be rare and demanded a group effort.

Oy Ihr Kleine Lichtelech (Morris Rosenfeld)
Oy ihr kleine lichtelech !
Ihr dertsehlt geshichtelech,
Meiselech ohn a tsohl;
Ihr dertsehlt fon blutigkeit
Biryeshaft un muthigkeit
Vunder fon amohl.
Ven ich zeh eich shminklendig
Kumt a chblom finklendig;
Redt an alter troim:
'Yid, du host gekriegt amohl,
Yid, du host ge-ziegt amohl,

Gott, dos gloibt zich koim.'
'S'iz bei dir a tolk geven
Bist a-mohl a-folk geven,
Ach, vie tief dos rihrt!'
Oy, ihr kleine lichtelech
Eiere geshichtelech,
Veken oif mein pein
Tief in hartz bevegt es zich
Un mit trehren fregt es zich
'Vos vet itz-ter zein?'

Oh you little lights
Tell such stories and
Numberless legends.
You tell of bloodshed,
Triumph and derring-do,
Those wonders of old.
When I watch you sparkle and glow
I feel revived.
An old dream comes to me:
'Jew, you fought before,
Jew, you once conquered.'
God, that's hard to believe!
You were once really something,
You were once such a people!
Oh how deeply that touches me.
Oh you little lights arouse
Such pain in my heart!
And with tears in my eyes
I ask what will happen now?

Morris Rosenfeld (Moshe Jacob Alter) died 22 June 1923. Translation *A Nos Amours*, with thanks to Rabbi Jeremy Rosen, Danielle Gilbert, Magdalena Wójcik, Keith Seward and Ann Malkin.

Unter Die Greeninke Boimelech (Chaim N Bialik)

Unter die green-in-ke boimelech
Shpielen zich Moishelech,
Shloimelecli,
Tsi-tsis kapotkelech, pealech,
Yidelech frish fon die ealech;
Gufimlech, shtroi, roich, un
federlech,
Nem un tsi bluz zei anf gliderlech,
(Chappen zei auf, gringe vin-te-lech,
Un es tsi-trugen zei fegelech; Oi!)

Under the budding branches
Little Moshe and Shlomo play.
Their Tsitzis, little coats and locks
Like freshly hatched eggs.
Young Jews, with their new eyes,
Young bodies like straw, smoke and
feathers: take them and blow them away.
Raise them and scatter them
Like little birds on the breeze, Oi!
Yet now only their little eyes remain,
Eyes like fading dots,
Shining and sparkling and piercing you.
Something of wonder is in them,
They reflect something inside you,
And you think of the days long gone,
Of the little birds.
Woe for my small Jewish children
And your holy little eyes, Oi!

Hayim Nahman Bialik (aka Chaim Bialik), died 4 July 1934. Translation *A Nos Amours*, with thanks to Rabbi Jeremy Rosen, Danielle Gilbert, Magdalena Wójcik, Keith Seward and Ann Malkin.

Traditional Yiddish Song

Oh, how quiet is the cemetery

Where no leaf is moving.

This world is sleeping sweetly.

If only he had kissed me!

His eyes are like black cherries,

His lips sweet as sugar,

If only he had kissed me!

Translation *A Nos Amours*, with thanks to Rabbi Jeremy Rosen, Danielle Gilbert, Magdalena Wójcik, Keith Seward and Ann Malkin.

Autour de Jeanne Dielman

Filmed on video camcorder in 1976 by Sami Frey on the set of *Jeanne Dielman, 23 Quai du Commerce, 1080 Bruxelles*; Edited by Agnès Ravez and Chantal Akerman; 70'.

Focusing on the on-set exchanges between star Delphine Seyrig and Chantal Akerman, witnessing the inception of the great work. A remarkable document.

Akerman 7

TOUTE UNE NUIT

BILLING

A Nos Amours continues a retrospective of the complete film works of Chantal Akerman with *Toute une nuit*, Akerman's tender, ever-restless nocturnal of 1982.

This is a film that begins at fall of night and ends as dawn approaches. Bathed in an Edward Hopper-like gloom of neon and tungsten bulbs, Akerman arranges and choreographs a series of brief encounters, wordless lovers' tender embraces, and the slow meanderings of lonely night owls.

These wordless interactions, often with musical interludes from jukeboxes and accidental sound (beautifully mixed by Jean-Paul Loublier, Akerman's regular collaborator, who also mixed *Jeanne Dielman*), accumulate into a wonderful screen dance, punctuated by stillness and silence. This is after all the realm of the insomniac and passing time is never so strongly felt.

'I want the viewer to physically experience the time spent in each shot. This physical experience of this time is in you; the film time unfolds in you' (Akerman has said). And as we all know, waiting for love, hoping for love, is all about time.

A Nos Amours is pleased to be co-presenting this screening with Birds Eye View Film Festival.

We are delighted that Richard Kwietniowski will introduce the film. Richard Kwietniowski made the very memorable *Love and Death on Long Island* and *Owning Mahowny*, and is a great admirer of Chantal Akerman.

BLOG

Chantal Akerman's *Toute une nuit*: to cleave and uncleave

HuffPo, 7 April 2014. See page 191.

THE HAND-OUT

Akerman 7: *Toute une nuit (All Night Long)*

This screening in the Chantal Akerman retrospective is co-presented with Birds Eye View Film Festival. Tonight's screening dedicated to the memory of Natalia Akerman, who died this month. Introduced by Richard Kwietniowski. Thursday 10 April 2014. ICA Cinema, 8pm.

Toute une nuit (All Night Long)

With: Natalia Akerman, Aurore Clément etc; Assistant directors: Liria Bégéja, Ignacio Carranza, Jean-Philippe Laroche, Pierre de Heusch; Cinematography: Caroline Champetier, François Hernandez, Mathieu Schiffman; Sound: Ricardo Castro, Henri Morelle, Daniel Deshays, Miguel Rejas; Design: Michèle Blondeel; Editing: Luc Barnier, Véronique Auricoste; Rerecording mixer: Jean-Paul Loublier; Foley artist: Jacky Dufour; Produced by Marilyn Watelet; 1982 35mm colour 1.66:1 89'; French, with English subtitles.

Akerman's choice of music is always a pleasure. She loved music and made her choices with particular care. One scene in bar features a song played on a jukebox, a song by singer-songwriter Véronique Sanson. It was inspired by the acrimonious end of Sanson's marriage to Stephen Stills. In another, a silly Italian pop song sings of love and forgiveness. But here too is a song from Mahler's *Kindertotenlieder*, setting Friedrich Rückert's poem mourning the loss of his children to scarlet fever, in this case the illusion that they might well yet return.

Ma Révérence (lyrics and Music by Véronique Sanson © Piano Blanc)
Quand je n'aurai plus le temps
De trouver tout le temps du courage
Quand j'aurai mis vingt ans

A voir que tout était mirage
Je tire ma révérence
Ma révérence
Quand mon fils sera grand
Qu'il n'aura plus besoin de moi
Quand les gens qui m'aimaient
Seront emportés loin de moi
Je leur tire ma révérence
Ma révérence

Et ma vie
Endormie
Doucement

Et mon cœur sera froid
Ne saura même plus s'affoler
Il ne deviendra qu'une pauvre horloge à réparer
Il n'aura plus de flamme
Il n'aura plus de flamme
Il n'y aura plus de femme

Et mes amis fidèles
Auront disparu un par un
Trouvant que j'étais belle
Que j'aurai bien fait mon chemin
Alors j'aurai honte de mes mains
J'aurai honte de mes mains

Quand je n'aurai plus le temps
De trouver tout le temps du courage
Quand j'aurai mis vingt ans
A voir que tout était mirage
Alors j'entends au fond de moi
Une petite voix

Qui sourd et gronde
Que je suis seule au monde
When I've run out of time
To find courage all the time
When the last 20 years
Will seem to be just a mirage
I'll take my bow
Take my bow

When my son grows up
And no longer needs me
When people who have loved me
All are gone
I'll take my bow
Take my bow

And my life
Gently
Slowing

My heart growing cold
Not knowing even how to get wound up
Something like a sad clock in need of repair
The flames gone out
The flames gone out
Nothing left of that woman

And my true friends
Disappearing one by one
Who thought that I was lovely
Who helped me on my way
Then I will be ashamed of my hands
I will be ashamed of my hands

When I've run out of time
To find courage all the time
When the last 20 years
will seem to be just a mirage
I hear now in the heart of me
A little voice
Welling up and growling
I'm all alone in the world

(translation Adam Roberts) With thanks to Warner Chappell Music.

L'amor perdonerà (performed by Gérard Berliner (aka Gino Lorenzi))
Love you know
Will forgive
Today you remain here
But why did you leave?
Love, you know
Will forgive.
But will it heal
This wound?
Because life
Has no more meaning,
My last love,
And if you don't love
You must leave.
I will not be able to
Begin again.
Love you know
Will forgive,
And only you
Can save me
Ahhhh
Love you know
Will forgive.
Even for us

There is luck,
The sweet life
And you are it.
Without you
I didn't exist,
I was with you ...to love
Love you know
Will forgive
Will forgive
Will forgive
Will forgive
Dooo be dooo

With thanks to Editions Amplitude for permission to reprint the lyrics and make this translation. Translation: Matteo Fargion.

Oft denk' ich, sie sind nur ausgegangen

From Kindertotenlieder, music by Gustav Mahler, text by Friedrich Rückert. The recording used is by Lucy Grauman (soprano) and Benjamin Rawitz (piano)

I think they've gone for just a moment
Soon will they be reaching back
Homewards in safety
The day is fine.
Oh, have no fear:
They merely go on a longer walk.
Indeed, they have but just gone out now,
And will be here at home in a moment
Oh, have no fear, the day is fine;
They merely go to walk on yonder heights.
They have gone out but all too early,
Unable now to find their house and return here.
We'll overtake them on yonder heights
In sun and shine, the day is fine on yonder heights.

Translation: David Paley, all rights reserved. Contact via *poemswithoutfrontiers.com*. Thanks to David Paley for permission to reprint.

Akerman 8

BILLING

A Nos Amours continues a retrospective of the complete film works of Chantal Akerman with *Les Années 80*, Akerman's extraordinary prototype adventure in the world of the MGM musical.

Perhaps because Godard had done it (with *Une femme est une femme*), as had Jacques Demy (with *Les Demoiselles de Rochefort*), so, too, was Chantal Akerman spurred to conceive of making a Technicolor musical. Or there again, maybe it is just the fact that Minnelli's musicals at MGM (how wonderful is *The Band Wagon*!) are such very good films that any film artist would want to navigate those waters. The trouble, in 1983, for Chantal Akerman was that a significant budget would be required. The solution, to put it crudely, was to make a 'making of' before the making, a kind of calling card that would beguile financiers.

Les Années 80 is that – but it is also an experiment, an adventure in intertextuality, the revelation of process that is in itself a search for a way of making. Chantal Akerman appears as herself, off and on camera, urging, instructing, commanding, performing. The spirit of her first film, *Saute ma ville*, is reignited – spritely, energetic and full of fun.

The beginning is a voice, speaking over a black frame: in the beginning was the word. At the close, the Jewish Seder's closing words are intoned: *next year in Jerusalem*. This is a film that offers the promise of that which is yet to come. In one sense that is that *Golden Eighties* would be successfully financed and made in 1986, but in another it is the unattainable object of desire which for an avant-garde artist must be forever distant.

Les Années 80 (1983, 82')

BLOG
Chantal Akerman's *Les Années 80*: a film about spinning
HuffPo, 24 April 2014. See page 194.

THE HAND-OUT
Akerman 8: *Les Années 80* (*The Golden Eighties*)
Thursday 24 April 2014. ICA Cinema, 7pm.

Les Années 80 (*The Golden Eighties*)
With: Aurore Clément, Magali Noël, Pascale Salkin, Michael Karchewski, An Nelissen, Yvon Vrioman, Samy Szlingerbaum, Amid Shakir; Script: Chantal Akerman and Jean Gruault; Song lyrics: Chantal Akerman; Cinematography: Michel Houssiau; Location sound: Marc Mallinus, Daniel Deshays, Henri Morelle; Re-recording mixers: Daniel Deshays, Olivier Boichard, Paul Bertault; Art department: Michel Boermans and Viviane Druez; Script supervisor: Eva Houdova; Editing: Nadine Keseman and Francine Sandberg; Music: Marc Hérouet; Produced by: Marilyn Watelet; 1983 35mm print colour 1.66:1 82'; French with English subtitles. Parts of this film were shot on video, but the closing sequence on 35mm. The two were married into a film print for screening.

MISCELLANEOUS
Adam Roberts' introductory remarks for *Les Années 80*
Shot on video and in the closing song and dance section on 35mm in 1983

The print today – 35mm, 82 minutes. In French with English subtitles

A script, of sorts, by Chantal Akerman…

… and Jean Gruault, a noted screenwriter with brilliant credits:

Rivette – ***Paris nous appartient***

Rossellini – ***La Prise de pouvoir par Louis XIV***

Godard – ***Les Carabiniers*** etc

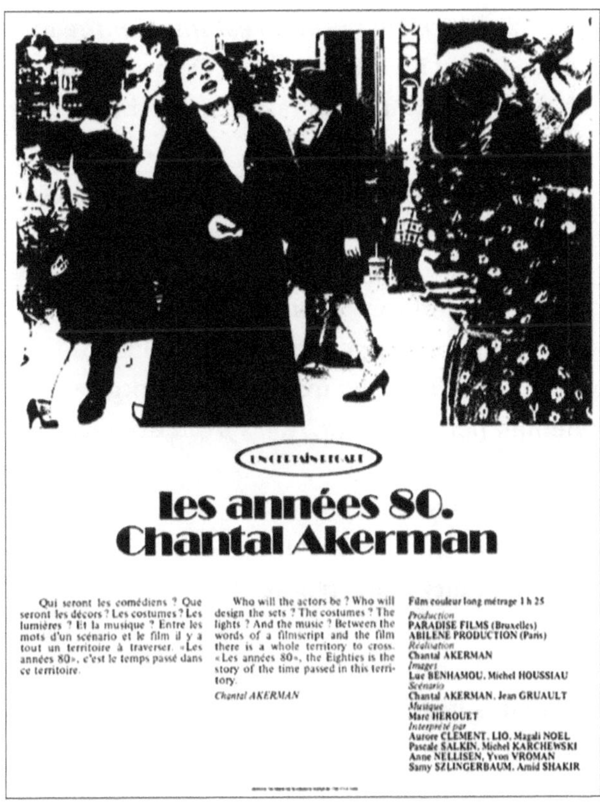

Cannes flier, for *Un Certain Regard*, 1983. Flier in private collection.

So Akerman is looking for a place in the mid-stream of European art-house cinema…

So what, in 1983, did Akerman want?

She had enjoyed brilliant success with *Dielman*.

She was a cineaste, a literate European who has studied with Levinas…

She was much admired by the most brilliant film theorists and cinephiles.

Godard liked what she did!

It was of course Godard with *Une Femme est une femme* in 1961, and then Jacques Demy in 1967 with *Les Demoiselles de Rochefort*, who had adored and then taken apart the Hollywood musical.

Why not? – the Hollywood musical is a wonderful thing.

How could Akerman, despite her seriousness, not want to do the same with this, her Eighties project?

She would have to raise significant finance: a musical such as she had in mind would require a large-scale studio build and 35mm cinematography – this from the maker of – to forgive the terms – experimental, perhaps dour, *News from home* and *Jeanne Dielman*

It was never going to be easy…

So Akerman made tonight's film – *Les Années 80*…

It's a making-of documentary made before the film it's about is made…

It's an experiment, an adventure in intertextuality, the revelation of process that is itself a discovery of a way of making.

And indeed, here she is: rehearsing, orchestrating, invigorating…

Akerman in the role of Chantal Akerman – the instigator, the energetic, energising principal, who can write the lyrics, conduct the recording, outdo the star…

Akerman appears as her manic herself, off and on camera, full of energy: urging, instructing, commanding, performing…

The spirit of her first film, *Saute ma ville*, is reignited – spritely, energetic and full of fun.

The beginning is a voice off, over a black frame: in the beginning was the word.

And at the close, the Jewish Seder's closing words are spoken: "next year in Jerusalem" – the promise of that which is yet to come.

L'shanah haba'ah biyerushalayim – prayerfully? Intentionally? Hopefully? Invocationally? With yearning? Trustingly?

Is that to be comfort had? Or is comfort deferred?

In one sense the promise of the Messiah and of Jerusalem is like *Golden Eighties* to come – the film that Akerman is here seeking to finance…

– but then, much too factually, she did indeed finance and shoot *Golden Eighties* in 1986…

… for me, in a key sense, the gesture of *Les Années 80* is more exciting – it is a gesture towards an unattainable object of desire …… which for an avant garde artist should be, must be, forever distant.

So in this sense, *Les Années 80* is the better film – the promise rather than the thing itself…

Akerman 9

UN JOUR PINA A DEMANDÉ &
L'HOMME À LA VALISE

BILLING

A Nos Amours continues a retrospective of the complete film works of Chantal Akerman with two shorter films from 1983: one a subtle study of the great, recently deceased choreographer Pina Bausch, and the other a delightful Kafkaesque comedy.

Introduced by artist film-maker and curator Lucy Cash.

We're also delighted to be joined by Chantal Akerman for this screening.

Un Jour Pina a demandé (One Day Pina Asked Me)

Dir. Chantal Akerman, France/Belgium 1983, 57'. With new translation and subtitles by Charlotte Maconochie.

Wim Wenders has recently made a film about Pina Bausch – but this film predates it by some decades, and is a very different object altogether. Comparisons will be intriguing.

Akerman and Bausch: two remarkable women makers. One is a maker of theatrical dance works, taking commonplace gestures and transforming them into extraordinary pageants, while the other is a maker of wonderfully choreographed compositions made of rhythmical everyday elements. Both offer an aesthetic that rearranges expectations of what matters. Both women have worked at the coalface of what women are dealing with, living with, and making the most of. The encounter is not a confrontation, it is a meeting of sensibilities, a perfect combination of a film-maker's sage framing of a dance-maker's flamboyant worldmaking.

L'Homme à la valise (Man with a Suitcase)

Dir. Chantal Akerman, France 1983, 60'. With new translation and subtitles by Charlotte Maconochie

A wonderfully wry and spritely comedy, in which Akerman plays herself returning from her travels only to find a man who had been staying in her apartment annoyingly is still in residence. Infuriatingly, he is writing, and writing prolifically as his noisy typewriter proves. Akerman meanwhile finds herself blocked. The tapping is a torment. A return to the physical performance of *Saute ma ville* and the opening part of *je tu il elle*, a perfectly realised existential comedy.

BLOG

Chantal Akerman: questions about duration

ICA Bulletin, 20 May 2014. See page 197.

THE HAND-OUT

Akerman 9: *Un Jour Pina a demandé & L'Homme à la valise*

Thursday 22 May 2014. ICA Cinema, 7pm. Introduced by artist film-maker and curator Lucy Cash. We are delighted to be joined tonight by Chantal Akerman.

Un Jour Pina a demandé… (One Day Pina Asked Me)

With: Pina Bausch and dancers of Wuppertal Tanztheater. Cinematography: Babette Mangolte and Luc Benhamou. Sound: Jean Minondo. Sound mix: Jean Mallet. Editing: Dominique Forgue and Patrick Mimouni. 1983 16mm transferred to video 57'. French with English subtitles. Translation Charlotte Maconochie

Gnädige Frau, Sie sind ja so schön, daß ich mich nicht trau, Sie anzusehn – Lovely lady, you are so beautiful that I dare not look.

Komm tanz mit mir, komm tanz mit mir, ich hab ne weiße Schürze für, lass nicht ab, lass nicht ab, bis die Schürze Löcher hat – Come dance with me, come dance with me: I've got a white apron on, don't leave off, don't leave off until the apron's quite worn out.

Richard Brody: Wim Wenders's *Pina...* is a European Cultural Product, a genteel and sumptuous packaging of great artworks that elides their fury to establish them on the altar of the cult of art-veneration that substitutes, in secular modernity, for religious submission.

Wenders is so devoted to Bausch's dances that he makes sure to catch everything. His camerawork and his editing are risk-free; he shows dancers making high-risk moves (the free falls and precarious balances in Bausch's work are nerve-racking to see) but he himself doesn't risk missing them. His framings and his cuts show, never hide, and to the extent that they do more than show, they mainly divert. By contrast, there is a prior documentary film of dances by Bausch, *Un Jour Pina a Demandé* (*One Day Pina Asked*), from 1983, in which the director, Chantal Akerman, films one of the dances that Wenders also features prominently in his film. The difference is apparent at once: Akerman doesn't show the whole stage, or even the whole action. Her tight framing on the woman being molested by men shows their bodies crowding her and their hands darting at her with what, for the viewer, is a complex musical rhythm but, from the woman's perspective, is an unpredictably harrying barrage. The duration of the shot is as aesthetically gratifying for a viewer as it is uncomfortably long for the woman. The composition gets to the heart of Bausch's dance by what it omits as much as by what it shows – by a framing that's as much an act of blocking out as of depicting.

The same is true of the circular processional steps that follow. An eye-level wide shot that seemingly begins as a relatively uninflected composition soon slices the circle into two arcs of dancers, the one in the foreground crossing in front of the other in the background, moving in opposite directions, creating a rhythmic visual counterpoint that – by concealing significant parts of the stage and of the action – reveals, analytically, incisively, one of the quiet aesthetic ecstasies of Bausch's art.

She uses the camera to reveal what the naked eye might not; she doesn't convey, she discovers.

Akerman is herself one of the greatest choreographic film-makers, as seen in her 1975 film *Jeanne Dielman, 23 Quai du Commerce, 1080 Bruxelles* and in her 1982 film *Toute une nuit (One Whole Night)*, which is even more dance-like in its delicately staged comings and goings than in its expressly danced sequences. Unfortunately, Akerman's film about Bausch hasn't been released here (even on home video); I caught it, by chance, on television in France about fifteen years ago (the best of all chances – flipping channels, having my eye captivated by something I couldn't identify, and watching with rapt attention to the end before finding out what I had been watching).

Of course, Akerman didn't have 3-D, and Wenders's film offers the intrinsic pleasure of seeing dance in perspective. But he doesn't do much more than preserve and transmit the dances – with admirable skill and care and a slightly heavy-handed wit. His filming of the dances is in the same spirit as the bland spoken tributes to Bausch that punctuate the soundtrack. Akerman's film is a work of modestly daring wonder, of exploration and inspiration. With her audacious compositions, decisive cuts, and tightrope-tremulous sense of time—and her stark simplicity – it shares, in a way that Wenders's film doesn't, the immediate exhilaration of the moment of creation. Akerman's film is of a piece with Bausch's dances; Wenders's is not.

(Richard Brody, *The New Yorker* December 12, 2011, reprinted with permission of Condé Nast.)

L'Homme à la valise (Man With a Suitcase)

With: Chantal Akerman, Jeffrey Kime; Assistant director: Jean-Philippe Laroche; Script supervisor: Eva Houdova; Cinematography: Maurice Perrimond; Foley: Jérôme Lévy; Location sound/rerecording mixer: Jean-Claude Brisson; Editing: Francine Sandberg; 1983 16mm transferred to video 60'; French with English subtitles; Translation: Charlotte Maconochie.

Sounds are coming from the room next door, from a room in Chantal's own apartment, made by a guest who just doesn't know when to go. Chantal has been away, expecting to find her house-sitter gone. He has other plans. Like Melville's extraordinary Bartleby, who to every reasonable request replies simply and irresistibly: "I would prefer not to". He is going nowhere. Chantal avoids confrontation, eating breakfast in her bedroom, attempting to co-exist. But his noises penetrate the walls, intruding on Chantal's attempt to concentrate and write, precluding the peace of mind that she needs and hoped for in her own home. Not quite Melville, then, but instead Kafka's mole-like creature in *Der Bau* whose cosy burrow is made into a living hell by untraceable sounds. The toilet flushes, bathwater splashes, feet pace, and the clatter of a typewriter shows the intruder is far from blocked. To even step out of the one room Chantal can call her own risks confrontation with the intruder, nude after taking a bath. But worst of all is his sing-song rendition of a song from *Oklahoma!* – the exclamation is correct, a mark of just how unbearable that folksy and saccharine world is.

Akerman herself plays her part to delightful comic effect, a return to the zest and wit of her arrival as a film-maker in *Saute ma ville*. As the comedy unfolds we are gently led into a world of multiple meanings, perhaps nothing less than a phenomenological parody of reason unhinged.

Akerman 10

FIVE SHORT FILMS

BILLING

A Nos Amours continues a retrospective of the complete film works of Chantal Akerman with five rare short films made in the 1980s. These films have not, as far as we can determine, ever been seen in the UK. These films are playful, daringly so.

J'ai faim, j'ai froid (1984) 12'

Two young Belgian women in Paris. They finish each other's sentences, they smoke each other's cigarettes: they are on the lam together. They are joined at the hip and ready for the challenges of the day – as women in the world – as long as they stick together. Spritely, playful, composed. Akerman has said, in an interview with Nicole Brenez, "My friend and I. A little musical comedy without singing." Is this film therefore autobiography?

Lettre de cinéaste (1984) 9'

A film-maker's self-portrait, asking hard questions of herself and of us. Invoking Aurore Clément as a kind of stand-in or proxy, a glamorous counterpart to Akerman who sports a drawn-on moustache. What is cinema for? Who is it for? If the Mosaic prohibition on making graven images includes film images, then where does that leave a Jewish film-maker?

Portrait d'une paresseuse (aka La paresse) (1986) 14'

A segment on sloth from a German TV commission on the theme 'Seven Women, Seven Sins'. As Akerman also told Nicole Brenez: 'Sonia (Wieder-Atherton) worked, while I stayed in bed'.

Again, Akerman mines her own life for material with which to weave her fine cloth.

Autour d'un marteau (1986) 4'
The hammer is the tool a sculptor uses to chip away at the block. It is the emblematic tool of French artist Jean-Luc Vilmouth, whom this film is ostensibly about. Akerman here instigates a game of musical chairs, as if the block is being chipped away. The winner is then permitted to hurl a hammer out into the starry night, where it whirls like the bone that becomes a spaceship in Kubrick's film.

Rue Mallet-Stevens (1986) 7'
In concrete terms, between 1926 and 1927 Robert Mallet-Stevens, a great architect of modernist inclination, made a set of Cubist houses in the 16th Arrondissement, on what was then named Rue Mallet-Stevens. This film, enigmatic, cryptic even, is set in that very street. A courting, or perhaps parting, couple cling to each other. A car approaches, its radio tuned to a station playing a song from *Golden Eighties*. What looks like a baby is brought out of a car by night, and taken into an apartment where a woman is playing a cello (Sonia Wieder-Atherton playing Dutilleux).

Four of these films are translated and subtitled for the first time by *A Nos Amours*.

THE HAND-OUT
Akerman 10: five shorts form the 1980s
Thursday 12 June 2014. ICA Cinema, 8pm.

J'ai faim, j'ai froid (1984)
Lettre de cinéaste (1984)
Portrait d'une paresseuse (1986)
Le marteau (1984)
Rue Mallet-Stevens (1984)

Why would a film-maker who had authored a series
of grand, large-scale structured works of superb control
take, in mid-career, to making shorts marked by playfulness,
self-referentiality, clumsy physical performance, an
avoidance of the potential of the retake to find perfection
of gesture, scrappy sound mix and edit, an informal
shooting style, and the apparently unmotivated inclusion
of elements that are not offered full explanation within
the confines of the work, thus making for a worrying sense
of inconclusiveness?

Perhaps because for Akerman the human body is not capable
of perfection: only its representation could be that. Akerman
makes clear (in *Lettre de cinéaste*, 1984) that such an ambition
would be a kind of paganism. In obedience to the Mosaic Law,
she claims to work not with representation but with textual
elements: she is woman of the Book.

Akerman in the 1980s was working tirelessly to bring
into being her musical *Golden Eighties* – a radical departure
that would alienate the fans of *Jeanne Dielman*. But the
author of *Jeanne Dielman* was also a film financier's
nightmare: too art-house surely to be bankable, too much
of a risk to undertak a mainstream feature film with a
large budget?

A work in progress project for *Golden Eighties* was released
in 1983, a kind of avant-garde taster reel (*Les Années 80*, shown
earlier in the retrospective). After this, while always working
towards the bigger project, short film commissions for TV and
vignettes for portmanteau films offered a chance to play. And
Akerman herself could enter the frame as a clownish presence,
stumbling, smoking, chatting, avoiding the elegant structures
and poised camera set-ups she was known for. Even scrappy
16mm cement film joins are sometimes allowed to show.
Hopefully, when restoration comes of these works (surely they
must!), that won't change.

What Akerman shows us in these very rarely screened
short films of the 1980s is fallibility, incongruity, obsession, a
somewhat gauche self, performance by stealth, a characterisation
and foregrounding of self as artist, as mistress of games, as
magician of the everyday, as radical realist, as exploiter of
zest and jouissance to animate her offer. Orson Welles's ludic
masterpiece *F For Fake* is perhaps a film in similar vein.

This evening's films run in chronological order.

J'ai faim, j'ai froid (I'm Hungry & I'm Cold)

With: Maria de Medeiros, Pascale Salkin, Esmoris Hanibal; Camera: Luc
Benhamou, Gilles Arnaud, Luis Peracta; Sound: François de Morant, Jean-Paul
Loublier; Editing: Francine Sandberg; Producer: Marc Labrousse; 1984 35mm b&w
12'; Live subtitles, translated and cued by Charlotte Maconochie.

A segment from omnibus commission: *Paris vu par... vingt
ans après* (*Paris seen by... twenty years on*) which premiered
in May 1984 at Cannes (*Un Certain Regard*). With the vigour
of a Nouvelle Vague film of the late 60s, two young women
quip their way on the streets of Paris, singing for their supper,
longing for love but finding boys less than equal to their
challenge.

Lettre de cinéaste (A Cineaste's Letter)

With: Chantal Akerman, Aurore Clément, Colleen Camp, Marilyn Watelet, Leslie
Vandermeulen, Lloyd Cohn; Camera: Luc Benhamou; Music: Marc Hérouet; 1984
video colour 8'; Projection format: digital; English subtitles, translated by
Charlotte Maconochie.

Cinéma cinémas was a legendary series of film programmes
broadcast on Antenne 2 (now France 2), curated by film-maker
Claude Ventura, journalist Anne Andreu and critic Michel
Boujut. *Cinéma cinémas* was serious and uncompromising. The
interview based editions could be brilliant, films in their own
right. *Cinéma cinemas* also commissioned essay films or self-
portraits from film-makers, and Akerman's film is one of these.

Cinéma cinémas (on air from 1982 to 1991) was, by the way, the inspiration and source for material for *Visions* on Channel 4 (1982 – 85) – which itself commissioned Akerman to make a short work: *Family Business* (1984), under similar carte blanche terms. *Family Business* will be shown on a later date.

Portrait d'une paresseuse (Portrait of a Sloth)

With: Chantal Akerman, Sonia Wieder-Atherton; Camera: Luc Benhamou; 1986 16mm colour 14'; Projection format: digital; Subtitled, translated by Adam Roberts and Louise Lyon.

A segment on a cardinal sin (sloth) from a German TV commission on the theme *Seven Women, Seven Sins*. As Akerman described it to Nicole Brenez: 'Sonia (Wieder-Atherton) worked, while I stayed in bed'. The film sets up two women in opposition: one active, vigorous, classical; the other chain-smoking, lazy, bed-loving, prevaricating. Of course Akerman is presumably both of these, since she knows all about the pleasures of idleness, and yet has been tirelessly productive. Again, Akerman mines her own life for material with which to weave her cloth.

Autour d'un Marteau – à propos Jean-Luc Vilmouth (Concerning a Hammer)

With: Jean-François Schneider, Camille Bordes-Resnais, Métilde Weyergans, Roberto Prual-Reavis, Danièle Bordes, Jean-Luc Vilmouth; Camera: Claire Atherton, Agnès Bruckert, Jacques Ulrich; Sound: Alix Comte; Editing: Claire Atherton; Sound mix: Alek Goosse; 1984 video colour 4'; Subtitled, translated by Jo Blair, with thanks to Charlotte Lopez.

The hammer is the tool a sculptor uses to chip away at the block. It is the emblematic tool of French artist Jean-Luc Vilmouth, whom this film is ostensibly about. One work Vilmouth made was a hammer fitted into a recess in the gallery wall – the tool as object. This work provides the opening image of Akerman's film. Akerman then instigates a game of

musical chairs, evoking perhaps how a block is chipped away
by a sculptor. The winner is permitted to hurl a hammer
out into the starry night, where it whirls like the bone that
becomes a spaceship in Kubrick's film. The words we hear
relate to Vilmouth's project: about habitation, about the idea
of habitation, of walls and the built environment, about the
concept of tool.

Rue Mallet-Stevens

With: Sonia Wieder-Atherton, Métilde Weyergans, Roberto Prual-Reavis, Coralie
Seyrig, Jean-François Schneider. Camera: Luc Benhamou. Sound: Alix Comte.
Editing: Claire Atherton. Cast: Chantal Akerman, Sonia Wieder-Atherton, Coralie
Seyrig. Video, 7', colour, projection. 1984 video colour 7' English subtitled.

Between 1926 and 1927 Robert Mallet-Stevens, a great architect
of modernist inclination, made a set of Cubist houses in the
16th Arrondissement in Paris. The street was then named Rue
Mallet-Stevens. This film, enigmatic, like a carnevale adventure,
suffused with romantic motifs, is set in that very street. A
courting, or perhaps parting, couple cling to each other. A car
approaches by night, its radio tuned to a station playing a song
from *Golden Eighties*. What looks like a baby is brought out of
a car, and taken into an apartment where a woman is playing
a cello (Sonia Wieder-Atherton playing Dutilleux). The close
brings Wieder-Atherton's bow and Akerman's rose together,
emblematic perhaps of off-screen romance.

Akerman 11

GOLDEN EIGHTIES

BILLING

Film collective *A Nos Amours* continues a retrospective of the complete film works of Chantal Akerman with an exuberant and sparky musical, at once homage to the Hollywood musical, and an expression of a highly European sensibility: satirical, teasing, resigned.

Introduced by film-maker Carol Morley (*Dreams of a Life*).

Chantal Akerman devoted enormous energy to this long-cherished project. Not only would she write and direct, but she also wrote the lyrics to the songs. Set in an other-worldly shopping mall called the Toison d'Or (which translates as The Golden Fleece), perhaps modelled on the mall of the same name in Brussels.

Golden Eighties interweaves tales of love, longing, disappointment and heartbreak. It offers song and choreographed – if not quite dance-like – movement. Akerman is working as ever with ordinary material, arranged and framed with precise purpose.

Meet Lili, proprietor of a hair salon, faithless lover, heartbreaker and opportunist. Meet Mado and Pascale, best friends, too kind to each other to share news of betrayal in love. Meet Sylvie, kept almost alive by letters from her lover far away in Canada looking for a fortune.

The musical numbers here touch on economic woes, recession, sexual positions, and can be catty and sarcastic – far removed from the sentimental world of MGM musicals, but not so far removed from the musicals of Jacques Demy or especially Renoir's odd valedictory song and dance segment in *Le Petit Théâtre de Jean Renoir*.

Shot with distinctive Fujicolor film stock, lit without shadows, stuck in an interior studio world as if exterior did not exist, jam-packed with infuriatingly catchy tunes, this is an astonishing work from an artist who began as a structuralist, albeit a structuralist with a gift for narrative.

Golden Eighties

dir. Chantal Akerman, France/Belgium/Switzerland 1986, 96', 35mm.

BLOG

Unfettered expression: Chantal Akerman's *Golden Eighties*

ICA Bulletin, 17 July 2014. See page 200.

THE HAND-OUT

Akerman 11: *Golden Eighties*

Thursday 17 July 2014. ICA Cinema, 7pm. Introduced by director Carol Morley.

Golden Eighties

With: Myriam Boyer, Delphine Seyrig, Fanny Cottençon, Pascale Salkin, John Berry, Nicolas Tronc, Lio, Charles Denner, Jean-François Balmer. Script by: Chantal Akerman, Leora Barish, Henry Bean, Jean Gruault, Pascal Bonitzer. Music: Marc Hérouet. Song lyrics: Chantal Akerman. Cinematography: Gilberto Azevedo, Luc Benhamou. Sound: Henri Morelle, Miguel Rejas. Script supervisor: Susy Rossberg Production design: Serge Marzolff. Re-recording mixer: Jean-François Auger, Alain Garnier. Editing: Francine Sandberg. Produced by Martine Marignac. 1986 35mm colour 96'. French dialogue. English subtitles cued by Charlotte Maconochie.

Marion Schmid: Golden Eighties is a perfect anthology of 1980s style: the satin skirts of the trainee hairdressers, Lili's red, low-cut dress and dangling jewellery, the large, tightly fitted belts, pink and pale-blue plastic raincoats, permed hair and red lipstick, all accessorise Akerman's hyper-stylised re-creation of 1980s consumer-culture chic. With its colourful costumes and setting, bright lighting, rapid editing arid quickly alternating song-and-dance numbers, the film displays an aesthetic of excess in stark contrast to the director's minimal, sober style of the preceding decade. *Golden Eighties* is a charming exercise in viewer seduction, an unashamed spectacle of femininity and a bold pastiche of melodrama and musical, the two genres which, as we have already seen in the context of *Les Années 80*, it uses as its thematic and aesthetic foil.

It is, above all, in the European rather than the American musical tradition, and especially in the line of Jacques Demy's musical comedies of the 1960s, that the film self-consciously positions itself. Demy, as Jill Forbes explains, 'first realised that the enclosed space of a gallery and its symmetrical design is the perfect foil for a musical, with the constraints of the setting justifying and shaping the choreography of the formation dancing, and making the musical romanticism seem more fantastic in contrast' (Forbes in *Sight and Sound*, 1987, 56, p145). In *Golden Eighties*, references to Demy's work abound: not only does the Galerie de la Toison d'Or appear as a postmodern avatar of the nostalgic turn-of-the-century passageways in his *Lola* (1961) (revealingly, in *Les Années 80*, Lili is still called 'Lola') but Sylvie's wall-less coffee bar resembles the bar-aquarium in in his *Demoiselles de Rochefort* (1967), with Sylvie herself evoking Mme Yvonne in the latter film, who prefers living in her dreams rather than confronting reality. The conflict between the commercially oriented parental generation and their offspring in quest of love, freedom and self-discovery, moreover, is reminiscent of Geneviève's (Catherine Deneuve) fate in *Les Parapluies de Cherbourg* (1964). In its self-conscious echoing of sets and themes, and its heightened melodrama and unashamed sentimentality, *Golden Eighties* pays homage to Demy's musical films. Like Demy, who raised ordinary spoken language to the status of song, Akerman makes extensive use of popular and youth culture in her self-scripted lyrics which are ingeniously set to music by Marc Hérouet. Schmaltzy love ballads quickly alternate with the a cappella mock songs of the group of 'bad boys' and the shampoo girls' giddy comments on passion and betrayal. The chorus deflates the romantic clichés that are lived and repeated by the central characters, its malicious comments distancing the spectator from the spectacle on display. More 1970s chanson than 1980s pop, the soundtrack nostalgically evokes Akerman's own youth at a time when the tunes of French composers and singers such as Michel Berger (author of the highly successful rock opera *Starmania*) and his wife, the Eurovision Song Contest winner France Gall, enjoyed international popularity.

If Demy and, more generally, the French tradition of using the emotional effect of song in modern cinema can be considered as crucial inspirations behind *Golden Eighties*, the film also engages in a playboy dialogue with the Hollywood musical whose conventions and values it playfully subverts. The traditional American musical, one of the most successful genres produced and marketed by the Hollywood studio system, follows a set of codes and strategies which, as Rick Altman and Richard Dyer have shown, underpin a coherent, subliminal ideology. Though rich in variations, the dominant model that emerged during the musical's heyday, roughly between 1930 and 1960, is characterised by a conservative social and sexual politics and a marked patriotism, manifest in its celebration of communal stability, advocacy of gender fixity and promotion of American wealth and, more generally, of the merits of capitalism. Traditionally based on a set of opposites – sex, age, social origin, temperament, values – it works through these binary oppositions with a view to abolishing difference in its resolution. Vincente Minnelli's *Gigi* (1958), as Altman has shown, is characteristic of the musical's paradigmatic structure: the marriage between the young, economically feeble Gigi to the older, wealthy Gaston that closes the romantic comedy merges what first appeared as irreconcilable opposites into a harmonious ending, promising prosperity and happiness for both lovers. Complicit with bourgeois value systems, the

Hollywood musical advocates marriage – Akerman calls it an
'ode to marriage' – as well as the traditional alliance of (male)
wealth and (female) beauty. 'The ecstatic, uplifting quality of the
musical's final scene', in the words of Altman, 'permits no doubt
about the permanence both of the couple and of the cultural
values which the couple simultaneously guarantees
and incarnates'."

(From Marion Schmid: *Chantal Akerman*, Manchester University Press 2010: p80ff.
All rights reserved. With thanks to Marion Schmid, Matthew Frost and Manchester
University Press for permission to reprint.)

Akerman 12

LETTERS HOME

BILLING

On 11 February 1963, Sylvia Plath, poet, author of *The Bell Jar*, thirty years old, married, with two children, killed herself. Then, in 1975, Aurelia Schober Plath, Sylvia's mother, published selected letters from her daughter as *Letters Home: Correspondence 1950 – 1963*.

These letters later provided the basis for Rose Leiman Goldemberg's off-Broadway hit: *Letters Home*. In 1984, this was staged in Paris, directed by Françoise Merle. In 1986 Chantal Akerman directed this video version.

Letters Home is therefore an object passed from a poet to her mother, from her mother to a woman playwright, then to a woman theatre director, and finally to a woman film-maker. This is a remarkable heritage: an object passed from hand to hand, a form of exchange between generations of mothers and daughters.

Hardly seen, but surely a work that elaborates Akerman's perpetual concern with communication and exchange between mother and daughter.

Introduced by film editor Claire Atherton who started working with Chantal Akerman in 1984 on *Letters Home*, the start of a long-standing collaboration on Akerman's fiction films, documentaries and installations.

Letters Home (1986 video 104' French, with English live subtitles, cued by Charlotte Maconochie.)

THE HAND-OUT

Akerman 12: *Letters Home*

Thursday 18 September 2014; ICA Cinema, 7pm. Introduced by Claire Atherton, Akerman's editor and collaborator.

Letters Home

Script: Rose Leiman Goldemberg, adapted from Letters Home by Sylvia Plath, edited by Aurelia Plath. Stage play direction: Françoise Merle. Video direction: Chantal Akerman. With: Delphine Seyrig, Coralie Seyrig. Camera: Luc Benhamou Sound: Alix Compte. Editing: Claire Atherton. Sound mix: Alek Goosse. 1986 colour video 104'.

Delphine Seyrig and her niece Coralie (daughter of Delphine Seyrig's brother Francis Seyrig, who composed the organ score for *L'année dernière à Marienbad*), showing themselves to the camera. Their words are those of Sylvia Plath, and of her mother. This is a correspondence between mother and daughter. Akerman knows about this sort of correspondence, and knows how to catch it on film.

The framings are front-on, in defiance of the cinematographic norm of reverse angles. Staging is not naturalistic, the props minimal, only as needed. These bodies are all too visible, close to, immediate. They are close to each other, close and very intimate.

Akerman wants to be near to these speaking mouths, the mouths that speak the words of mother and daughter. The words, like the soul's very own breath. The words reassure. "Maman, Maman, I'm fine," repeats the daughter, over and over.

Akerman looks at the effect of words, not the speaking, and not the hearing, but somewhere in between. She is an artist of our times, of suspicion, rents, broken meanings. She wants to find the cracks in the structure, the fault lines. The bodies of a mother and daughter are there, before us, smiling, beautiful, like columns, upright and plausibly strong. They can see each other of course, look at each other, but if they look at the camera, they are not looking at a machine, but at us…

The mother-daughter dyad is at the root of Akerman's film-making. Like Proust (how Akerman loves and knows Proust!) she registers the pangs and vicissitudes of complex, ambivalent exchanges between mother and daughter, sees how the need for mutual understanding between a mother and daughter can be so fraught and complex. Recall the scene in *Les Rendez-vous d'Anna* when mother and daughter lie side by side in bed, reunited, and how what they share, with such hope of comfort, is all to no avail. Hence, perhaps, the importance of letter-writing. Letters written at a remove, at some distance; from mothers to daughters and from daughters to mothers.

Letters Home, shot on video, presents a play that began life away from the camera. It seems simply to want to preserve the theatrical staging of Françoise Merle's Paris production (in 1984 at Théâtre Moderne). It is beautifully performed. It is a decidedly refined affair. And yet it is all the same deeply unsettling, evoking turmoil and unhappiness. What is this, this dread, this presentiment of disaster? What is so alarming about freedom?

No doubt because the film-maker registers the two voices, their need and their piercing dependence, composing something like a fugue, the two voices separate and yet intertwined. A mother knows there is little she can truly do to protect, or perhaps to forge her daughter, and a daughter knows that she is fated always to struggle in a search her for true self, fated never to really find the true essence of herself alone.

(A paraphrase inspired by Laure Adler's text from *Autoportrait en cinéaste* (Éditions du Centre Pompidou/Éditions Cahiers du Cinéma, Paris 2004: 197. Laure Adler could not be contacted so that the fine original could be given.)

Akerman 13

HISTOIRES D'AMÉRIQUE

BILLING

Histoires d'Amérique was shot in New York, conjuring up a specific diasporic context – not dissimilar to that of Woody Allen's masterpiece *Broadway Danny Rose*. This may be the new world, but the horror of the old is never far from the surface. Mordant observation and biting cynicism rule.

Akerman asked her cast to re-create jokes, fables and anecdotes, culled from real-life testimony, sashaying from the comical to the tragic, interleaving all with slapstick humour that only Jewish New York knows how to do. As Akerman said: when history becomes impossible to bear, there is only one thing to do: send yourself up and laugh.

Histoires d'Amérique

Cast: Maurice Brenner, Carl Don, David Buntzman, Judith Malina, Eszter Balint, Dean Jackson, Roy Nathanson. 1989, 92'.

BLOG

Laugh or cry: Jewish humour in Chantal Akerman's *Histoires d'Amérique*

ICA Bulletin, 22 October 2014. See page 202.

THE HAND-OUT

Akerman 13: *Histoires d'Amérique (aka American Stories: Food, Family and Philosophy)*

Thursday 23 October 2014. ICA Cinema, 7pm. Introduced by artist film-maker Ruth Novaczek. With: Maurice Brenner, Carl Don, David Buntzman, Judith Malina, Eszter Balint, Dean Jackson, Roy Nathanson. Camera: Luc Benhamou. Sound: Alix Comte.

Editing: Patrick Mimouni. **Sound** mix: Gérard Rousseau. 1989 35mm transferred to video 92'.

Marcel Jean: The intelligence of Chantal Akerman's latest film, *Histoires d'Amérique*, lies in the exactitude she brings, facing her characters full-on, gazing upon them with a plain, open regard, respectfully but discreetly, without a trace of emotionalism. *Histoires d'Amérique* is essentially the story of Jewish immigration from Central Europe to the east coast of the United States. The tales and memories which Akerman presents are complementary but inseparable, ranging from the tragic (tales of pogroms, Holocaust and exile) to the comic (the irrepressible humour of Jewish New York with its existential angst).

On the one hand, Akerman captures in long, static framings, revelling in their real time, a series of short biographical accounts delivered to the camera by motionless characters. These are tales characterised by discomfort, anxiety, sadness but sometimes also serenity. On the other, again favouring a fixed camera, with the front-on point of view familiar to us throughout her career (think of *Toute une nuit* or *Un Jour Pina a demandé*), accepting that she will record them in real time, Akerman frames characters performing a series of sketches distilling the essence of New York Jewish humour.

By alternating the tragic and the comic, refusing to explain, something extraordinary emerges clearly, as naturally and inevitably perhaps as night following day, a picture of individual and collective tragedy, expressed with a singular sense of humour, the masque of despair, facilitating (perhaps) escape.

We know that Akerman has always had an affection for New York; indeed her work has been deeply influenced by the structuralism of the underground films of the 60s (think of *Hotel Monterey*, her first feature-length film, and her remarkable *News from home*, both are proof of that).

Moreover, it is pertinent to remember the burlesque elements found elsewhere in Akerman's films, such as in *L'Homme à la valise*, *Golden Eighties* and the audition sequences in *Les Années 80*. *Histoires d'Amérique* is thus in several regards a return to a familiar place and a bridge between modes of film-making.

Akerman's great talent for simple staging and shooting, her familiar asceticism, which is fundamentally in character Warholian, serves to uncover the simple sincerity of emotion, to make apparent without recourse to classical dramatic representation. Moreover, we can think of *Histoires d'Amérique* as a work close in sprit to *Toute une nuit*, another film of raw emotion, another nocturnal film, another film refusing conventional narrative or dramatic impetus, another film of multiple destinies, crossroads and outcomes.

And again, to set *Histoires d'Amérique* alongside another of Akerman's films, it appears as a happy aesthetic counterbalance to *Golden Eighties*. That is to say, with this film, the autobiographical tendency of *je tu il elle* is transcended – it is instead an invocation, a film stripped of the merely personal, an exploration of collective memories and narratives. She is drawing on her influences, and sticking to her conception. Even in the soundtrack she includes quotes and fragments from previous work, rather than present, motivated sounds. Her choices are personal, never narcissistic. *Histoires d'Amérique* is the work of a mature film-maker. It is a rare and beautiful film, aspiring to an absolute purity and coming close to achieving it.

Toute la mémoire du monde by Marcel Jean. 24 images, n° 46, 1989, p. 83 (Montreal). Translation Adam Roberts. With thanks to Bruno Dequen, Marcel Jean and Revue 24 images for permission to reprint.

Akerman 14

THREE FILMS

BILLING

Les Trois dernières sonates de Franz Schubert (1989, 49')
Alfred Brendel, one of the greatest of all pianists, plays and
reflects on Franz Schubert's last three piano sonatas. As he
points out, Schubert can't have known that he was soon to
die, so they probably do not embody the air of resignation and
finality future generations have sentimentally insisted they bear.
They were, however, long neglected, all but forgotten, and
only in more recent times have they come to be treasured and
performed. The repose and wisdom of the maestro, together
with the patient observation of one who is no stranger to the
idea of the irrevocably lost, of the erasures of history, and of
the value of fragile objects passed carefully from generation to
generation, are a joy.

Trois strophes sur le nom de Sacher (1989, 12')
The first of Chantal Akerman's collaborations with cellist
Sonia Wieder-Atherton. Here Wieder-Atherton performs Henri
Dutilleux's *Strophes*, composed between 1972 and 1986. These
are ethereal, at times hesitant, but lyrical pieces.

Le Déménagement (1992, 42')
It is worthy of Beckett: 'I should never, never have moved. What
got into me? I was happy before. Well, almost. No, mostly I was
not. Not good at all. I had to move.' The man in his new home,
unable to unpack the many boxes and crates that surround
him. His soliloquy is one of indecision, of regret, of a sense
of predicament that is inescapable. Through this protagonist,

Akerman reflects on the impossibility of making decisions, of the forlorn hope of certainty.

BLOG

Chantal Akerman: film-making as composing.

HuffPo, 11 November 2014. See page 204.

THE HAND-OUT

Chantal Akerman 14

Trois strophes sur le nom de Sacher (1989)

Les trois dernières sonates de Franz Schubert (1989)

Le déménagement (1992)

Thursday 13 November 2014. ICA Cinema, 7pm.

Trois strophes sur le nom de Sacher
(Three stanzas on the name 'Sacher')

With: Jean-Christophe Bleton, Francesca Lattuada, Sylvie Seidmann. Camera: Rémon Fromont. Sound and mix: Nicolas Joly. Designer: Pierre Jaccaud. Editing: Rose Legrand. 1989 video 12'.

Chantal Akerman collaborates with cellist Sonia Wieder-Atherton, who here performs Henri Dutilleux's beautiful, haunting *Strophes* of 1972. The music was commissioned by the cellist Mstislav Rostropovich to mark the 70th birthday of the Swiss conductor Paul Sacher. Sacher was a hugely influential and key figure in 20th century music, who used his wealth to commission key works, from the likes of Bartók and Stravinsky. The music is said to be 'on the name Sacher' as it derives its material from a musical cryptogram: Es (E♭), A, C, H, E, Re (D). Dutilleux asks for unusual tuning of the cello, producing the specific sound world of the Strophes. The film might be contrasted with Hitchcock's *Rear Window* for its dramatic use of windows and disjointed narratives.

Les trois dernières sonates de Franz Schubert (Franz Schubert's Last Three Sonatas)

Interviewer: Mildred Clary. Director of photography: Jean Monsigny. Cameras: Jacques Pamart, Michel Lecocq. Location sound: Xavier Vauthrin. Editing: Francine Sandberg. Sound mix: Jean-Yves Rousseaux. Originated on video. Television commission for Arte's Opus series, curated by Mildred Clary. 1989, 46'.

Alfred Brendel, one of the greatest of all pianists, plays and reflects on Franz Schubert's last three piano sonatas. Brendel has done more perhaps than any other to promote and champion Schubert's work.

To quote Brendel's own biographical note: he was not a child prodigy, his parents were not musicians, there was no music in the house, and he is neither a good sight-reader nor blessed with a phenomenal memory. Brendel had little conventional music training, certainly none after the age of 16. Indeed, Brendel relates that he was given a ReVox tape recorder on which he began to record pieces he was studying, listen to himself and so react. He has long advocated and performed Schubert, pointing out that, unlike the great architect Beethoven, Schubert "strides across harmonic abysses as though by compulsion".

Why did Akerman make this film? Is Schubert's music, with its superficial simplicity, its felicities, its extremes of shifting mood, and its melancholy, the ideal soundtrack to her own project?

Le Déménagement (The Move)

With: Sami Frey. Assistant director: Thomas Cheysson. Script supervisor: Isabelle Ribis. Camera: Rémon Fromont. Sound: Alix Comte. Editing: Rudi Maerten. Sound mix: Gérard Lamps. Produced by Sophie Goupil. Television commission for La Sept's Monologues series. 1992 35mm transferred to video 42'.

Ivone Margulies: Frey's monologue can be seen as a special form of naïveté, a pose or mimicry of innocence or simplicity that constitutes a form of irony between the verbal and the dramatic. Verbal irony is a form of speech in which

one meaning is stated while a different, often antithetical
meaning is intended; dramatic irony is a plot device in which
the protagonist behaves inappropriately or unwisely and
the spectators know more than the protagonist, observing
a contrast between what the protagonist understands about
his acts and what the text demonstrates about them. Falling
between verbal and dramatic irony, *Le Déménagement*
presents Akerman's text in a desiccated cinematic shape:
could the man's monologue be as well served onstage? Or as
part of a book? Not quite – the weight of Akerman's writings
and dialogue-qua-monologue is... intrinsically related to its
performance, to her oblique displacements of the agencies
of narration. Yet the fact that in *Le Déménagement* it is the
text that almost single-handedly carries the burden of her
categorical oscillations is crucial.

As Frey sits in a chair, facing the spectator, the camera
tracks in on him. This is the sum of the cinematic devices of
Le Déménagement. Made for a TV series entitled *Monologues*,
the film has a theatrical setting that reduces the dialogue-
qua-monologue strategies of films like *Les Rendez-vous
d'Anna* and *Jeanne Dielman* to bare, antinaturalistic effects.
Le Déménagement plays mostly with words, and because the
arbitrariness of the verbal sign makes it less malleable than
the photographic image, the film seems to be clearly making a
case against the illusions of referentiality. The theatricality of
Frey's frontal confessions is another sign of anti-illusionism –
yet this theatricality ultimately becomes the stage for a moral
condemnation of the character. Instead of arguing for the
arbitrariness of signs, the mise-en-scène of Frey's solitude
creates a strangely naturalising twist. Given the ambivalence
of the film's scene, we wonder whether this gesture toward
reflexivity is another bluff, another tactical manoeuvre from a
film-maker who often plays by simulation. But the character's
naïve confusion of the three women fits in with Akerman's

habitual desire for referential instability and is finally unco-optable by her knowing authorial nod here.

One can suggest, in fact, that even in Akerman's most coherent simulations (*Jeanne Dielman*, *je tu il elle*), the consistency between the films' cinematic structures and their characters' pathologies at some point breaks down and shows as fissure. Conversely, one can add that it is Akerman's formal liminality – her delay in framing eccentricity, in distinguishing subject from object, texture from theme – that allows for the greatest gains in active spectatorship. The issue for Akerman, as for other film-makers after Godard, remains that of the reflexive strength of mimicry. Is her double-layered mimesis a particular form of reflexivity, or are we moving into a different representational dimension? The most conspicuous trait of Akerman's aesthetic is the categorical blur it promotes. Her anti-hierarchical effects depend on a perverse notion of the copy, one that even ventures into making actual references. These effects are also, and significantly, contingent on a slowing down of tempo, a different perceptual temporality, and an acute detour from the open-endedness common in European art films of the 60s.

(From Ivone Margulies: *Nothing Happens: Chantal Akerman's Hyperrealist Everyday*, 1996 Duke University Press: 209-210. With thanks to Diane Grosse and Duke University Press for permission to reprint.)

Akerman 15

BILLING

This screening is introduced by the renowned critic Olaf Möller.

Julie (Londez) and Jack (Langmann) are a provincial couple in love who have only just moved to Paris. Home is a small flat, a nest for young lovers. By day they make love, while at night Jack drives a taxi, and while he drives that Julie walks the warm summer streets, singing happily to herself.

They meet Joseph (Négret), another newcomer to the city, driver of Jack's cab by day. Julie falls for Joseph. Julie now has lovers around the clock. Julie resists making a choice. Why should she? She can even happily, dreamily make do without sleep. Is night better than day, or vice versa?

Picking up on the insomnia and nocturnal pacing of *Toute une nuit* and *Les Rendez-vous d'Anna*, but finding a new ease and musical cadence to the marking of time and measuring out of gestures that seems quite composed and song-like. Perhaps Akerman is channelling the mysterious and other-worldly patterns of Fred Astaire and Cyd Charisse dancing in the dark in Central Park (in *The Band Wagon*, of 1953). In any case, this is a remarkable, ravishing film, full of brilliance.

Nuit et Jour (1991, 90')

THE HAND-OUT

Akerman 15: *Nuit et Jour (Night and Day)*

Thursday 11 December 2014. ICA Cinema, 7pm. Introduced by Olaf Möller.

Nuit et Jour (Night and Day)

With: Guilaine Londez, Thomas Langmann, François Négret, and the voice of
Chantal Akerman. Screenplay: Chantal Akerman and Pascal Bonitzer. Director of
photography: Jean-Claude Neckelbrouck. Production design: Dominique Douret,
Michel Vandestien,Costume designer: Brigitte Nierhaus Location sound: Alix
Compte. Script supervisor: Agathe Sallabery. Editing: Francine Sandberg. Foley:
Marie-Jeanne Wijckmans. Music: Marc Hérouet, with Sonia Wieder-Atherton, Michel
Vandestien. Re-recording mixer: Gérard Lamps. Produced by Marilyn Watelet, Pierre
Wallon. 1991, 35mm print, colour, 1.66:1 90'. French, with live English subtitles
translated and cued by Charlotte Maconochie.

Ginette Vincendeau: Whereas many contemporary French
films, such as *Un monde sans pitié* (1989), *Les Amants du
Pont-Neuf* (1991), Rohmer's *Les Rendez-vous de Paris* (1995)
and *Chacun cherche son chat* (1996), have tried, within the
constraints of shooting in today's Paris, to make the living
city a 'real' character, *Nuit et Jour* proposes a self-consciously
distanced city, one that is turned into a set. This is symbolised by
the view outside Julie and Jack's apartment window, evocative
of the 1930s Poetic Realist films. But Akerman also turns the
'real' city into a set. The long backtracking shot of Julie and
Joseph standing in front of the statue at the centre of the Place
de la République is emblematic of this: it starts off on a real
exhibit of Paris history (as well as on the two characters), only
to detach itself from this referent, the circular movement of the
cars around the square increasingly filling the frame, a series
of blurred movements and lights. Joseph's recitation over the
two-minute-long shot is a poetic discourse on the everyday, in
the tradition of poet and scriptwriter, Jacques Prévert. Joseph's
text tells us what he likes about Paris. It evokes the quotidian
pleasures the cosmopolitan city offers its inhabitants, such as
eating cous-cous in Belleville; drinking café-crème; shopping for
toothbrushes, cigarettes or pistachio nuts; going to the cinema;
reading the newspaper at café terraces; taking the Métro. These
are activities which the film will deliberately not show us, but
which Akerman acknowledges as part of the cinematic heritage

of the city, a heritage so culturally familiar that it can be reduced
to this verbal rendering.

Julie and then Julie and Joseph walk Parisian streets as if
on an empty set, the outdoor equivalent of Julie and Jack's
apartment. While being undoubtedly the real city, Paris in
Nuit et Jour is offered as a disembodied, self-conscious
representation, illustrated by Julie's singing 'Moi, la nuit j'erre
dans Paris' ('At night I wander around Paris'), as she is walking
the streets, a reference to Jacques Demy's musicals. As in the
Demy films, this also signals another dimension conferred onto
the city by Akerman's film, and that is its "magic".

Early French cinema widely used the streets and buildings
of Paris for naturalistic purposes, but the city also inspired
directors who endowed it with a surreal, magic dimension.
This is evident in Louis Feuillade's serial fantastic thriller, *Les
Vampires* (1915 – 16), and in avant-garde fantasies such as René
Clair's *Paris qui dort* (1924). The 1930s, especially in the early
films of Clair, such as *Sous les toits de Paris* (1929), and the
tradition of Poetic Realism, produced a stylised view, literally
reconstructing the city with sets, which derived poetry from the
minute observation of the everyday. Akerman acknowledges
this tradition by placing Julie and Jack's apartment in a popular
quartier, on the 5th floor "without a lift", under the roofs
of Paris. Poetic Realism also retained a dimension of magic,
illustrated by the presence (sometimes literally as a character) of
"fate" in the films. The New Wave introduced a more "authentic"
city, based on the practice of location-shooting. Paris, not yet
utterly dominated by traffic, allowed actors and film-makers the
exhilaration of exploring the city as a playground – literally in
Truffaut's *Les Quatre cents coups* (1959) – or metaphorically in
so many others: *A bout de souffle* (1960), *Les Cousins* (1959),
Paris vu par... (1964), as well as the locus of self-discovery
and danger – Varda's *Cléo de 5 à 7* (1961), Godard's *Vivre sa
vie* (1962) and others. But, even then, the magic dimension

of the city was retained: Truffaut wondered at the function
of the pneumatique as a device to connect lovers in *Baisers
volés*; Rivette staged elaborate plots across the city in, among
others, *Céline et Julie vont en bateau* (1974) and *Le Pont
du Nord* (1981); and Rohmer's *Conte d'hiver* (1992) makes
long-estranged lovers meet again by divine chance on a bus.
French auteur films in the 1980s and 1990s continue this trend
– notably Olivier Assayas's *Irma Vep* (1996) and Rochant's
Un monde sans pitié (1989). The former, the story of a failed
attempt at filming a remake of *Les Vampires*, features a scene in
which "Irma Vep" (Maggie Cheung) steals jewels from a hotel
room and throws them down in an eerily poetic – yet location-
shot – rooftop scene. *Un monde sans pitié* puns on the idea of
magic with a scene in which the hero "switches off" the Eiffel
Tower for the woman he loves by clicking his fingers at the exact
moment (midnight) when the lights go off.

The Paris of Julie and Joseph, like the fairy-tale apartment of
Julie and Jack, is a magic city, with an endless supply of hotel
rooms, squares and fountains, in which nothing unpleasant can
happen, especially to Julie as she wanders the streets at night on
her own ('nothing happened to her', confirms the voiceover)
with her "magic shoes" which she throws away at the end. It is
a city which exists for the lovers and in relation to them, and in
which golden coaches are replaced by taxis. It is noticeably a
city free of inhabitants. When other characters might have been
present – for instance, when Julie buys shirts, or when either
Julie or Joseph sits in a café waiting for the other – they are
cut off, metonymically replaced by fleetingly seen hands or the
anonymous backs of their heads. The only encounters the lovers
make in *Nuit et Jour* are with cars, but these, too, are, as in the
Place de la République sequence, mostly blurred movements
and lights, brushing past the lovers as they stand on the edge
of the pavement, or seen from Jack's moving taxi on the night
he takes Julie with him. As in *Les nuits fauves* (1992), *Boy*

Meets Girl (1984), *Les Amants du Pont-Neuf* (1991) and many others, a new motif – strings of light filing past as a car is riding in a tunnel – has been added to the visual repertoire of the modern city. Jack and Joseph as taxi-drivers are no longer the friendly, comic taxi-drivers of classical French cinema (as played by Michel Simon or Louis de Funès), but part of a new breed of shadowy characters prowling the city – as in Jacques Bral's *Extérieur, nuit* (1979) – part of it, yet distanced and stripped of the social identity that such an occupation would normally suggest, emblematic of the stylisation of the whole city.

(From: *Night and Day: a Parisian fairy tale*, Ginette Vincendeau, in *Identity and Memory: The Films of Chantal Akerman* ed. by Gwendolyn Audrey Foster, Flicks Books, Wiltshire, 1999: 125. With thanks to Ginette Vincendeau, Gwendolyn Audrey Foster, Matthew Stevens and Flicks Books for permission to reprint.) With thanks to Charlotte Maconochie for revising comprehensively a very poor translation and for cueing the live subtitles.

Akerman 16

D'EST

BILLING

D'Est (*From the East*) **is a** wordless winter travelogue through the
countries of Eastern Europe, from East Germany, through Poland
and the Baltic states, across Russia towards Moscow and its
cavernous terminal stations. The Soviet era has gone, its collapse
leaving behind a seemingly stunned, endlessly waiting populace.

   The film begins with a series of late summer images, at
the beach, or lazing in the park. Winter threatens. Long lines
of anonymous people, suggestive of resignation and an
unfathomable fortitude. Akerman's camera tracks these lines,
catching the stamp of frozen feet, the hunch of shoulders bearing
the cold. Domesticity life is a silent one, though sentimental songs
can be played on a gramophone and may be company of a sort.
Sausage and bread and salt are on the supper menu for one. Even
the grand terminal stations of the capital serve only to lend the
waiting crowds a new kind of insignificance.

   Bleak, for sure, but beautiful image-making and laying out
of materials, the deft and caring work of a great artist. It is hard
not to think of Samuel Beckett in this absorbing study of human
futility, especially the exchange from Endgame: Clov: "If I don't
kill the rat, he'll die"… Hamm: "That's right."

L'Est (1993, 110')

BLOG

Travelling shots in Chantal Akerman's *D'Est*.
HuffPo, 21 January 2015. See page 208.

THE HAND-OUT
Akerman 16: *D'Est (From the East)*

Thursday 22 January 2015. ICA Cinema, 7pm. Introduced by Keifer Taylor, *A Nos Amours* blog editor.

D'Est (From the East)

Assistant director: Szymon Zaleski. Cinematography: Rémon Fromont, Bernard Delville. Sound: Pierre Mertens, Thomas Gauder, Didier Pêcheur. Editing: Claire Atherton, Agnès Bruckert. Produced by Helena Van Dantzig, Marilyn Watelet. Tchaikovsky violin suite played by Natalia Shakhovskaya. 1993 16mm blown up to 35mm 110'.

Steven Ball: ... To haunt does not mean to be present, and it is necessary to introduce haunting into the very construction of a concept. Of every concept, beginning with the concepts of being and time. That is what we would be calling here a hauntology. Ontology opposes it only in a movement of exorcism. Ontology is a conjuration.[1]

"Hauntology" is a concept that has travelled some distance over the 20 years since the publication of *Specters of Marx*; developed by cultural critics such as Mark Fisher and Simon Reynolds to become associated primarily with musical forms of the contemporary representation of the past.[2]

As well as being the year in which *Specters of Marx* was delivered and published, 1993 is also the year in which Chantal Akerman made *D'Est*, a film that presents its own spectres as a (coincidental) parallel enquiry to Derrida's interest in the immediate aftermath of Soviet communism. Akerman started her journey in East Germany, arriving eventually in Moscow; it was "a voyage Chantal Akerman wanted to make shortly after the collapse of the Soviet bloc 'before it was too late'"

1 Jacques Derrida, *Specters of Marx: The State of the Debt, the Work of Mourning and the New International*, trans. Peggy Kamuf, Routledge, New York, p. 202
2 e.g. *Fisher k-punk* blog (*http://k-punk.abstractdynamics.org/*); Reynolds, *Ghosts of Futures Past: Sampling, Hauntology and Mash-ups, Retromania: Pop Culture's Addiction to its Own Past*, Faber and Faber, London, 2011, pp. 311-61.

Akerman recognised that something would soon pass and
from her travels made an elegiac, impressionistic documentary
around this transitional moment. From images of peasants
planting crops, driving through flat, agrarian lands, tracking
around snowy streets, we see large groups of people standing,
apparently waiting. Maybe they await a new life, perhaps a loaf
of bread, perhaps what was to come after perestroika – the
deconstruction, as Derrida might have it – in the wake of the
glasnost, the newly decreed openness, the brave new socio-
political condition they were supposed to live in? The grandeur
of railway stations and restaurants become settings for an
apparently displaced population. We see tableaux filmed in
people's homes, in their kitchens, as they prepare food, and
play sentimental music redolent with nostalgia... for what? For
the Cjust past, or for an absent partner or child? We will never
know, as life seems weirdly both quotidian and in suspension,
time seems out of joint.

Akerman makes no commentary; she allows the scenes to
speak, or perhaps to not speak, for themselves; lack of contextual
information coupled with the individuals' inscrutability gives little
away in this slow, measured flow of impressions.

Akerman claims that her approach was to shoot what she saw,
ostensibly without an agenda, using the slow, steady camera
tracking or the static shot as the circumstance demanded, as the
generous duration of the film might allow its context to emerge.
'In my films I follow an opposite trajectory to that of the makers
of political films,' she once said. 'They have a skeleton, an idea
and then they put on flesh: I have in the first place the flesh, the
skeleton appears later.'[3] This corporeal metaphor again suggests
a formulation of hauntology, Derrida's "movement of exorcism"
or ontology as "conjuration". But what actually is conjured in

3 Akerman quoted in David Schwartz, *Bordering on Fiction: Chantal Akerman's Journeys Through Time, Space, and History*, *Moving Image Source*, July 2008: *http://www.movingimagesource.us/articles/bordering-on-fiction-20080702*.

D'Est? Is there an essence here receded from view that is never fully appreciated from appearances, a cause never fully deduced from the effect and its apparition?

Akerman's plan to make the film "before it was too late" begs the question: too late for what exactly? Perhaps before the society formed under Soviet cdisappears. In this sense the people in this film may have already been spectral presences, always already ghosts conjured from a past time, and now, 20 years after the event, even more so. We see them only ever in passing, without the agency of a voice to speak for themselves, and if they do it is in Russian, untranslated. And, as the title with its cardinal, directional specificity would seem to assume a Western audience, like the spectre they withdraw from contact with their intended audience. The haunting doubles. There is the spectre of Soviet communist society, but are its people or the ghosts of its people the ghosts of communism? Perhaps. Marx's core materialist conception is that social being determines social consciousness, and in terms of historical materialism a society "does not consist of individuals, but expresses the sum of interrelations, the relations within which these individuals stand". In *D'Est* we are seeing a society in the form of relations with a crumbling state apparatus, and in the 20 years since the film was made Russia has become a major global capitalist economic force. Marxism and radical leftism, however, maintain their influence on Western thought. Slavoj Žižek, for example, perhaps one of the most public of contemporary philosophers, has expressed his commitment to communist ideals, while acknowledging that the analysis of communism must always focus on its failure. But Derrida already suggested in 1993 that the "failure" of communism is not fatal:

Capitalist societies can always heave a sigh of relief and say to themselves: communism is finished since the collapse of the totalitarianism of the twentieth century and not only is it finished, but it did not take place, it was only a ghost. They do no more than disavow the undeniable itself: a ghost never dies, it remains always to come and to come back.[4]

And so now, 20 years after it was made, *D'Est* returns the Soviet Union to us: the ghosts come back not just as a memory of Soviet communism after communism, its subjects, and the places they inhabited, but also as revenant political formulation. The film's refusal of explicit commentary, its remove from its subject, its even pace, could now be considered not so much an elegy, as I suggested above, but producing time for speculative reflection on that what haunts the 21st century is perhaps the possibility of what communism might have been, and what it could still be.

(Thanks to Steven Ball for permission to reprint. Extracted from an article originally published in *Senses of Cinema* (2013): *www.sensesofcinema.com/2013/cteq/ dest-spectres-of-communism/*. Steven Ball is an artist who works in a range of audiovisual media. He also writes about moving image art with a particular interest in post-landscape and post-colonial representations of place and space. He is currently Research Fellow at Central Saint Martins, University of the Arts, London.)

4 *Derrida*, 1993, p. 123.

THREE SHORT WORKS

BILLING

Family Business (1984, 18')

Every film-maker must raise money for their project. The author of *Jeanne Dielman* is no exception. Here Akerman travels to Los Angeles, in search of a rich uncle who may have a cheque book and feel like financing a movie. He may be rich, but can he be found?

Akerman's friend Aurore Clément welcomes her to L.A. but really just wants help rehearsing for her latest part. The battle to pronounce 'cheated' without the inevitable mispronunciation of a French speaker takes up all their time and energy. Aurore's American companion, another actress, complains bitterly about the casting process, usually a matter of risky, intimate meetings late at night. In any case Akerman hears her uncle has just left for New York. Like Alice, Chantal must chase her white rabbit.

Ecrire contre l'oubli (Writing against forgetting, aka ***Pour Elizabeth Velásquez, El Salvador)*** (1991, 4')

Commissioned by Amnesty International as part of a portmanteau project to highlight the fate of the murdered, the detained and the tortured. Akerman's contribution is dedicated to an El Salvadorian trade unionist, a mother of three, murdered by the US-backed junta. Catherine Deneuve emerges from the calm of a Parisian night to deliver a heartfelt plea for the significance of Febe Elizabeth's life, so that she be remembered, not least for the sake of her orphaned children. Sonia Wieder-Atherton's cello weeps appropriately.

***Portrait d'une jeune fille de la fin des années 60 à Bruxelles** (aka **Portrait** of a Young Girl from the Late Sixties in Brussels)* (1993, 60')

To quote Judith Mayne, who exactly captures the delightful manner and audacity of this delicious film:

Chantal Akerman's 1993 film… is a beautiful and haunting evocation of female adolescence and its discontents, including desire, loss and the complicated, ambiguous relationship to the transitions between girlhood and womanhood… *Portrait of a Young Girl* is in many ways a coming-out story, for the love of one girl for another moves the film forward… But it will come as no surprise to those familiar with Akerman's work that this is no transparent coming-out tale, and that the film resists any of the simple oppositions between inside and outside, past and present, before and after, which are suggested by the very term 'coming out'.

Rather, this explores how lesbian desire is both shaped and repressed by the codes and conventions of heterosexual romance. On the surface, the film could be described as a somewhat conventional girl-meets-boy tale. But what shapes the girl-meets-boy story is the simultaneous desire, for the girl, to connect to another girl and to tell stories. In other words, this is a lesbian narrative with a difference; girl still meets boy, but that classical and timeworn plot is the pretext for the connection between two girls.

(From: *Identity and Memory: The Films of Chantal Akerman*, Gwendolyn Audrey Foster, Flicks Books, Wiltshire, 1999: 150. With thanks to Judith Mayne, Matthew Stevens and Flicks Books for permission to reprint.)

THE HAND-OUT

Akerman 17: three short works

Thursday 12 February 2015. ICA Cinema, 7pm. Introduced by John Ellis, who commissioned Akerman's *Family Business*. John Ellis is now Professor of Media Arts at Royal Holloway, University of London.

Family Business (1984)

Commissioned by Channel 4 *Visions* strand. With: Aurore Clément, Colleen Camp, Chantal Akerman, Marilyn Watelet, Lloyd Cohn, Leslie Vandermeulen. Camera: Luc Benhamou. Editing: Patrick Mimouni. Music: Marc Hérouet. 1984 16mm transferred to video colour 18'. English and French dialogue, with some subtitles.

Ecrire contre l'oubli (aka Pour Elizabeth Velásquez, El Salvador) (1991)

Commissioned by Amnesty International. With: Catherine Deneuve, Sonia Wieder-Atherton. Director of photography: Joan Monsigny. Camera operator: Arthur Cloquet. Sound recording: André Rigaut. Editing: Pascal Marzin. Sound mix; Gérard Lamps. Music: Mino Cinélu. Cello: Sonia Wieder-Atherton. Produced by Béatrice Soulé. 1991 35mm French with English subtitles 4'. Translated by Charlotte Maconochie.

Portrait d'une jeune fille de la fin des années 60 à Bruxelles (Portrait of a Young Girl from the Late Sixties in Brussels) (1993)

Commissioned as part of the TV series: *Tous les garçons et les filles de leur âge.* Cast: Circé Lethem, Julien Rassam, Joëlle Marlier, Cynthia Rodberg. Camera: Rémon Fromont. Sound: Pierre Mertens. Assistant director: Patrick Quinet. Script supervisor: Corine Bachy. Editing: Martine Lebon. Sound editors: Christiane Weil, Zofia Menuet. Sound mix: Gérard Lamps. 1993 Super 16mm transferred to video 60'.

Marion Schmid: Akerman's 1993 film *Portrait d'une jeune fille de la fin des années 60 à Bruxelles* (hereafter *Portrait d'une jeune fille*) is part of a television series entitled *Tous les garçons et les filles de leur âge (All the boys and girls of their age)* commissioned for the French national arts channel La Sept/ Arte. Nine directors of different age groups, including, amongst others, Claire Denis, André Téchiné and Olivier Assayas, were invited to film an autobiographically inspired tale of adolescence set against the backdrop of their own teens. Based on personal memories, the series was thus designed to reflect the spirit, atmosphere and socio-political make-up of the recent French past stretching from, roughly the early 1960s to the early 1990s. Beyond the focus on adolescence, the film-makers were required to use music from the period in question, to include a party scene, to respect the medium format of a 60-minute film and to work within a limited budget (5.4 million francs per film). The opening credits of Akerman's film posit its temporal frame as April 1968, that is, just one month before the student revolts in Paris which 'function as a mythical origin story in narratives of the new Left, a poststructuralist theory and film culture' (Jerry White, Chantal Akerman's Revisionist Aesthetics 2008: 417). By virtue of 'being not quite Paris, not yet May' (ibid.), the film's setting decentralises the revolutionary spirit from the capital to a periphery, thus fitting the autobiographical remit required by the series whilst at the same time extending its scope from a strictly metropolitan French to a European Francophone context.

The film chronicles one day in the life of Michèle (Circé Lethem, the daughter of Belgian experimental director Roland Lethem, acknowledged as Circé' in the credits), a teenager ill at ease with herself and the world who has decided to quit school as her first act of revolt against the parental generation (her first spoken words are an ominous "Au revoir, papa"), the strictures of repressive morality and traditional gender roles and the boredom of social conformism. At the movies, she meets Paul (Julien Rassam), a young deserter with whom she strolls along the city's boulevards, talking, shoplifting, kissing...

Coming of age and youthful rebellion are, of course, favourite themes of French cinema – one may think of Truffaut's classic *Les Quatre cent coups* (1959) or, more recently, Claude Miller's *L'Effrontée* (1985) and Catherine Breillat's *36 fillette* (1988) and *À ma sœur!* (2001) – and, as such, they were not altogether new to Akerman, who had offered original studies of adolescence in works such as *Saute ma ville*, *je tu il elle* and her 1984 *J'ai faim, j'ai froid...* that follows the journey of two teenage girls who run away from Brussels to Paris. The vicissitudes of love and friendship and the quest for sexual initiation, both important themes of *Portrait d'une jeune fille*, are among

the standard topoi of this popular sub-genre and thus rather
predictable in terms of genre convention. Where Akerman can
be seen to innovate on the coming-of-age narrative is in grafting
upon the more conventional heterosexual encounter that is the
staple diet of this type of film, the tale of one girl's attraction
for another, and in showing the complex ways in which the
relations with the female love-object are fashioned by the
heterosexual norm.

MISCELLANEOUS

Ecrire contre l'oubli – the subtitles

00:48   Writing Against Forgetting

00:54   Mr Alfredo Félix Cristiani, President of the Republic of
San Salvador, El Salvador

00:57   Febe Elizabeth Velásquez, killed for her trade union
activities in a bomb blast.

01:06   Febe Elizabeth Velásquez was killed on 31 October 1989.

01:12   in a bomb blast.

01:14   She was prepared for it, she knew it could happen
to her.

01:20   No more shared kisses, no more impromptu meetings.

01:23   No more daybreak, no more dawn.

01:25   They eliminated you.

01:27   They murdered you.

01:32   Your voice fell silent, your eyes closed.

01:35   Febe Elizabeth Velásquez, they left you there, lying in
the debris.

01:40   And with you, nine others.

01:43   And with you, nine others.

01:47   Your smile, Febe Elizabeth Velásquez
01:51   Oh, that fearless smile.

01:54   They murdered her, they eliminated her, but didn't erase her.

01:58   They couldn't erase her.

02:01   She, Febe Elizabeth Velásquez,
02:04   she dared to think, she dared to be, she dared to smile.

02:09   She once was. She is no more.

02:13   She once was. She is no more.

02:18   They left you there, lying in the debris.
02:20   With nine others. Nine others.
02:23   Your smile lives on, Febe, in the hearts of those who loved you…
02:27   still love you… and will continue loving you.

02:31   She, Febe Elizabeth Velásquez,
02:35   she dared to think, she dared to be, she dared to smile.

02:40   Her smile lives on,
02:42   Febe, in the hearts of those who loved her, still love her... and will continue loving her.

02:52   They eliminated you but not from our memories.
02:55   They eliminated you and nine others, and there will be more and more.
02:59   Torture, screams, tears, separated families.

03:02   Enough.
03:03   Enough.

03:05   Ruins, dust, fresh blood… enough.

03:09   They eliminated you.
03:11   They eliminated you but not from our memories
03:14   but not from our memories.
03:15   They eliminated you and nine others like you.
03:18   Nine others.

03:23   And there will be others like you, or different
03:28   who will think like you
03:30   who will dare to be someone, Febe Elizabeth Velásquez
        de San Salvador
03:34   and who will dare to be someone.

03:38   Febe Elizabeth Velásquez, with that bright and
        courageous smile,
03:43   bright and infectious.
03:46   Your voice fell silent, your eyes closed,
        you are at rest already.

03:52   You, Febe Elizabeth Velásquez de San Salvador
03:56   your face, your courage and your name, we will
        keep them
03:59   We will keep your smile, they couldn't erase it.
04:04   It is here inside me, for evermore, for evermore, inside
        me for evermore.

04:15   [credits]

Akerman 18

**_LE JOUR OÙ & UN DIVAN À NEW YORK_
(A COUCH IN NEW YORK)**

BILLING

***Un Divan à New York** (A Couch in New York)* (1996, 105')
The plot reads like the outline of a film from another age: a dour
New York psychoanalyst Henry (William Hurt) decides to house
swap his Fifth Avenue apartment for a place in Paris. He ends
up in the bohemian home of a dancer named Béatrice (Juliette
Binoche). She is insouciant as he is dour, and messy as he is tidy.
Henry's patients love Béatrice, and she finds she really can help
them. Coming home, Henry finds his world in superb shape.
Even his dog is happier. Henry has the wit to lie on her couch.

Akerman's confection has a lightness that is hard to catch if
in a hurry. Good to watch some Lubitsch beforehand to get into
the mood. Peter Bogdanovich summarised the Lubitsch touch,
but might have been talking about *Un Divan à New York*:

"Something light, strangely indefinable, yet nevertheless
tangible… one can feel this certain spirit; not only in the tactful
and impeccably appropriate placement of the camera, the
subtle economy of his plotting, the oblique dialogue which had
a way of saying everything through indirection, but also – and
particularly – in the performance of every single player, no
matter how small the role."

Le Jour où (1997, 7')
Akerman told Nicole Brenez in her Lola Pyjama Interview in
2011 that it is "at its heart, a homage to Godard". A return then
to her roots, as her first film, *Saute ma ville*, was made with
Pierrot le fou in mind. This is Akerman again having a lot of fun.

Akerman 18: *Le jour où... & Un Divan à New York*
(A Couch in New York)

Thursday 12 March 2015. ICA Cinema, 7pm.

Le Jour où... (The Day When)

Cinematography: Rémon Fromont. Location sound: Nicolas Lefebvre. Editing: Claire Atherton. Colour grading: Patrick Crucy. Sound mix: Pascal Vuillemin. Produced by Silvia Voser. A film by Chantal Akerman. 1997 35mm colour 7'. French with English subtitles, translated by Adam Roberts and Ian Monk.

Cybelle H McFadden: Akerman revisits a similar investigation later in her career In the film *Le Jour où...* She uses the same format as the one in *La Chambre*: the circular panoramic without cuts, six and a half times around the room, shows a limited space repeatedly. The form mirrors the circular and reflexive content. She reads a text over and over again, and this emphasises the usual repetition of the film. Akerman's presence is especially important. since she not only shows herself in front of the camera, but also reads a highly reflexive text about the future of cinema, entitled *Le jour j'ai pensé à l'avenir du cinéma (The Day I Thought about the Future of Cinema)*. She repeats the text, and this repetition exists on the sentence and thematic levels as well...

The day Akerman decides to think about the future of cinema ends up being a bad day for her, including a keyboard malfunction of the "e" that marks words as feminine in French. Significantly, gender specificity related to artistic creation is perturbed for her, which underscores ambivalence about her status as a female film-maker... The camera movement and the repetition of the images reflect the circularity of her thoughts. Akerman uses this enacted reflexive mode of address in her self-portrait: she describes her artistic task – creating her self-portrait – in a circular way so that she ends where she really wanted to start in the first place."

(From Cybelle H. McFadden, Gendered frames, embodied cameras: Varda, Akerman, Cabrera, Calle, and Maïwenn, 1975. With thanks to Cybelle H. McFadden, Patricia Zline, Fairleigh Dickinson University Press for permission to reprint.)

Le Jour où
Un film de Chantal Akerman

Le jour où j'ai décidé de penser à l'avenir du cinéma

Je me suis levée du mauvais pied
J'ai versé un jus de pamplemousse sur un verre retourné
J'ai laissé mon bain déborder
J'ai renversé le café d'un geste large
J'ai mis mon T-shirt à l'envers
Je n'ai pas repris ma monnaie chez le marchand de tabac
J'ai payé mes cigarettes sans les prendre
J'ai appelé mon chien qui n'est pas venu
J'ai reçu une carte pour mon anniversaire et j'ai pleuré
J'ai répondu au mauvais téléphone quand il a sonné
Le E de mon clavier s'est coincé et j'ai pensé, j'ai pensé à lui
mais sans me rappeler son nom
Après je m'en suis souvenue, il s'appelle Georges Perec
Pensait-il a l'avenir de la littérature quand il écrivait
Je me suis dit qu'il est mort parce qu'il fumait trop
J'ai immédiatement écrasé ma cigarette dans mon cendrier et
sans plus attendre j'en ai allumé une deuxième
J'ai téléphoné à l'amie qui m'a envoyé la carte et je suis tombé
sur quelqu'un d'autre
J'ai dit excusez-moi je ne suis pas réveillée.

Le jour où j'ai décidé de penser à l'avenir du cinéma

Je me suis dit que je ne le verrais pas
Je me suis demandée si l'avenir c'était toujours devant soi
Alors j'ai regardé devant moi puis je me suis retournée

Je me suis demandée si les gens qui marchaient la tête penchée
avaient le sens de l'avenir ou si c'était seulement les gens qui
marchaient fièrement et la tête droite.

Je me suis dit que pour moi l'avenir était derrière moi parce
qu'on ne dit plus de quelqu'un de mon âge qu'il a un bel avenir
devant lui.

Le jour où j'ai décidé de penser à l'avenir du cinéma, je me suis
donc levée du mauvais pied.

Quand on se lève du mauvais pied on ne peut pas penser

Et certainement pas à l'avenir du cinéma

Quand on se lève du mauvais pied on ferait mieux de ne pas se
lever

De ne pas se verser du jus de pamplemousse

De ne pas se faire couler un bain

De ne pas se faire du café

Et surtout de ne pas appeler son chien

Quand on se lève du mauvais pied

Faut pas avoir son anniversaire

Ni téléphoner

Encore moins penser à Georges Perec, et à sa littérature

Et encore moins dire aux gens qu'on est pas encore bien éveillé

Quand on se lève du mauvais pied

Vaut mieux se recoucher

Si par hasard on se réveille et qu'on pense sans y penser

à quelque chose qui vous passe sans que vous le sachiez dans

votre tête bien éveillée et qui oublie qu'elle doit penser, on
se réjouit

tout d'un coup parce qu'on se dit qu'il se pourrait bien que

demain, après demain où un jour qui vient on verra bien
quelque

chose dans le noir et on le saura, ce sera un beau morceau de

cinéma.

Répétition du début...

Le jour où j'ai décidé de penser à l'avenir du cinéma

Je me suis levée du mauvais pied
J'ai versé un jus de pamplemousse sur un verre retourné
J'ai laissé mon bain déborder
J'ai renversé le café d'un geste large
J'ai mis mon T-shirt à l'envers

The day I decided to think about the future of cinema, I got out
of the wrong side of the bed.
I poured grapefruit juice onto an upside-down glass.
I let my bath overflow.
I knocked over my coffee with a sweeping gesture.
I put my T-shirt on inside out.
I didn't pick up my change at the tobacconist's.
I forgot my cigarettes after paying for them.
I called my dog but he didn't come.
I got a card for my birthday and I cried.
I answered the wrong phone when it rang.
The E on my keyboard got stuck. I couldn't remember that
writer's name.
Then it came back to me, it's Georges Perec.
Was he thinking about the future of literature when he wrote?
I recalled that he had died because he smoked too much.
I stubbed out my cigarette immediately, then immediately lit up
another.
I phoned the friend who had sent me the card but found it was
someone else.
I said, excuse me, I'm not yet awake.
The day I decided to think about the future of cinema

I said to myself that I wouldn't see it.

I wondered if the future lay always ahead.

So I looked in front, then turned around.

I wondered if people who walked leaning forward had the same sense of the future as people who walked head proudly aloft.

I thought that for me the future must be behind me, because people of my age are never told that they have a glittering future in front of them.

So, the day I decided to think about the future of cinema, I got out of the wrong side of the bed.

When you get out of the wrong side of the bed, you can't think and certainly not about the future of cinema.

When you get out of the wrong side of the bed, you'd do better by not getting up, not pouring yourself some grapefruit juice, not running a bath, not making coffee, and especially not calling your dog.

When you get out of the wrong side of the bed, don't have a birthday and don't call anyone.

And especially don't think about Georges Perec and about writing.

Or tell people that you haven't woken up yet.

When you get out of the wrong side of the bed, you should go back to bed.

If by chance you wake up and think, without thinking, about something that unbeknown to you has crossed your wide-awake mind, which forgets that it shouldn't be thinking, you find this quite delightful, and say to yourself that it may well be that tomorrow, or the day after tomorrow, or someday soon, you'll see something in the dark, and you'll know that this is a beautiful piece of cinema.

(Thanks to Silvia Voser and Waka Films for permission to reprint. Translation Adam Roberts and Ian Monk.)

Un Divan à New York (*A Couch in New York*)

With: Juliette Binoche, William Hurt, Stéphanie Buttle. Written by Chantal Akerman, Jean-Louis Benoît. Cinematography: Dietrich Lohmann. Production design: Christian Marti. Sound recording: Pierre Mertens. Editeing: Claire Atherton. Music: Sonia Wieder-Atherton. Sound mix: Gérard Lamps. 1996 35mm 1.66:1 108'. English and French.

A game of opposites: tidy/messy, male/female, French/New Yorker, ordered/intuitive, cool/hot, chaotic/ordered, extrovert/introvert, noisy/quite etc... A buttoned-up psychoanalyst is brilliant – and yet his patients stop dreaming under his care. Even his dog has symptoms. But wherever Parisian dancer Béatrice (her name being that of Dante's muse is no coincidence) steps, she leaves traces, and changes lives. The motherly containment she offers the psychoanalyst's patients soon cures them, and even the dog is changed for the better. Enigmatically, about this film, Akerman said, "death of my father" (in the notes she gave Nicole Brenez in the *Lola Pyjama Interview*).

MISCELLANEOUS

The introduction given by Joanna Hogg and Adam Roberts
Today we present a short and a feature film. The short has hardly been seen at all and the feature has suffered from reviews that misunderstand it badly.

The short will play first, and the hand-out gives you a transcription of the text that Akerman herself delivers. This is a film that harks back to *La Chambre* that she made in New York decades previously, though there are significant differences – as you will see. We are very grateful to Waka Films for the loan of the print.

The feature film follows – and we must apologise for the subtitles – French and Dutch – but this is apparently the last runnable 35mm copy. Beyond that, however, it is in pretty good condition, and the cinematography shines through. This film has been mauled by some mainstream critics: which should serve as a warning against critics!

We think some of the poor criticism illustrates well what a film (any film) can be up against – worth noting that these views are likely read by audiences BEFORE they even see the film!

The *New York Times* said this:

Though not noted for her humor, the film-maker Chantal Akerman has attempted light romantic comedy in *A Couch in New York* … And though this 1995 film has been discussed in terms of Lubitsch, Cukor and Capra, it has a premise that could work for Neil Simon, too…. It takes a while to get past the strained, wide-eyed ingenuousness of *A Couch in New York*, in which the film-maker's solemn side and Mr. Hurt's own gravity are never out of reach. (Ms. Binoche, though playing dumb with extravagant naïveté, is at her most radiant and soothing.) But eventually this lightweight fable develops its charms. As photographed by Dietrich Lohmann, it has a glossy visual sophistication, and the score, including much cello music, by Sonia Wieder-Atherton (who has worked on several other of Ms. Akerman's films) has its lulling refinement, too. And once the film moves past its initial vapidity, it takes on a reasonably blithe aura of romance. Still, nothing, from the film's mischievous notions about psychoanalysis to its ideas of culture shock, has much weight. Coming from Ms. Akerman, this is pleasant but unaccountable fluff.

And *Variety* said this:

Belgian director Chantal Akerman and stars William Hurt and Juliette Binoche are not names automatically associated with screwball romantic comedy, and *A Couch in New York* illustrates why. Spun from the rather pedestrian premise of a cross-cultural meeting of opposites who attract, and saddled with dialogue only a screenwriter's mother could love, this lifeless, mostly

studio-shot confection of amour and analysis rarely puts a
foot right... Hurt and Binoche appear awkward in their roles,
and the gradual melting of his aloofness and her spontaneity
into a middle ground where sparks ignite is achieved rather
mechanically. Binoche especially appears out of place; while
the French thesp has consistently held her own as an intense,
solemn beauty in pics such as *The Horseman on the Roof*,
"Damage" and *"Three Colors: Blue,"* her casting as an adorably
irresponsible kook stretches credibility to the limit.

The worst must be *Time Out*:

Akerman's most overtly commercial project yet turns out to
be a comedy without humour, a romance without affection. She
laboriously hauls into place all the items on the specification:
wacky premise (dancer Binoche pretending to be a psychiatrist,
psychiatrist Hurt pretending to be a patient), best friends to
whom the plot can be confided, a big cute dog. But it never
begins to come to life. Hurt looks haggard, Binoche flutters
prettily, a butterfly in a graveyard. The prevailing gloom is lifted
only by some imaginative art direction.

BY: BBA (who is BBA?)

But the *San Francisco Chronicle* said this:

Romantic comedies that do more – such as *A Couch in New
York* – are rare. This lovely, lilting picture... doesn't follow a set
pattern, and it's about more than simply two people who find
each other. It's about the mysteries of attraction and different
ways of looking at life.... In *A Couch in New York*, two people
explore each other's apartments, then each other. It's a process
of discovering their own incompleteness and, at the same time,
the cure. It's a movie that's at once coolly thoughtful and wildly
romantic. The acting is a marvel. Both Binoche and Hurt are
superb at conveying the big emotions in mere half-sentences,
and Ackerman makes good use of the close-up. That Hurt is an

internal, introspective actor is hardly news, but so is Binoche. In the midst of Beatrice's cascades of dialogue, it's possible to see her thinking, switching gears, changing her way of expressing herself, careful not to hurt anyone.

At last, a review with some awareness of the strategies and regimes of this postmodern homage to screwball. This, to our mind is a film that brings to mind Mitchell Leisen, Lubitsch, Capra…

Imagine, if you will, that instead of Hurt and Binoche you are watching William Powell and Jean Arthur… it will all come clear. Hope you agree.

Akerman 19

CHANTAL AKERMAN PAR CHANTAL AKERMAN & SUD

BILLING

Chantal Akerman par Chantal Akerman & Sud

Introduced by Dr Muriel Tinel-Temple.

Chantal Akerman par Chantal Akerman (1996, 63)
Commissioned as part of the series: *Cinéma, de notre temps*
  The legendary series of film-maker portraits curated by Janine
Bazin and André Labarthe offered Akerman a commission. She
chose, perhaps not unsurprisingly, to make a study of herself as
film-maker. Why not? She had turned film-making back on itself,
and discovered a feminised and 'other' sensibility, another way
of seeing the world and self.
  Akerman delivers a monologue about her work and
thinking. This is followed by a montage of clips from her
work, including *Jeanne Dielman*, *Saute ma ville*, *Hotel
Monterey*, *Histoires d'Amérique*, *Toute une nuit*, *Portrait d'une
jeune fille de la fin des années 60 à Bruxelles*, *Les Années
80* and so on.
  Akerman closes with a simple statement of fact, without
biographical adornment: "I was born in Brussels, that's
the truth."

Sud (South) (1999, 71)'
Inspired by a love of writing by William Faulkner and James
Baldwin, Akerman planned a meditation on the American
South, perhaps to be modelled on her film *D'Est*. But, just
as she began work, James Byrd, Jr. was murdered in Jasper,
Texas. A black man, he was severely beaten by three white men,

chained to their truck, and dragged three miles through a black neighbourhood until he was dead.

Akerman's engagement is not mere reportage. Jasper, the context for the crime, is scrutinised. Patient interviews reveal the people and their attitudes. Byrd's funeral is a moment of deep feeling.

This is a film that finds an alternative to the forensic investigation of, say, *In Cold Blood*. This is a film that evokes a terrain, the folds of a psychological condition, the cold heart of white supremacism and the extraordinary nobility of the black community under attack.

Perhaps it is Akerman's sense of exclusion, stemming from her family's experience of the Holocaust, that enables her to see in this way.

Akerman has written:

How does the Southern silence become so heavy and so menacing so suddenly? How do the trees and the whole natural environment evoke so intensely death, blood, and the weight of history? How does the present call up the past? And how does this past, with a mere gesture or a simple regard, haunt and torment you as you wander along an empty cotton field, or a dusty country road?

THE HAND-OUT

Akerman 19: *Chantal Akerman par Chantal Akerman & Sud*

Thursday 23 April 2015. ICA Cinema, 6.40pm. Introduced by Dr Muriel Tinel-Temple.

Chantal Akerman par Chantal Akerman

Commissioned by Janine Bazin and André Labarthe for *Cinéma, de notre temps*. Camera: Rémon Fromont and Philippe Gilles. Sound: Xavier Vauthrin. Editing: Claire Atherton. Sound mix: Francisco Camino and Laurent Thomas. 1996 Betacam SP colour 63'. French with English subs + English.

The best way to make this self-portrait would be to let my films speak for themselves... I'd edit them together and create a new film which would then become a portrait of myself.

La meilleure manière de réaliser cet autoportrait ce serait de faire parler mes anciens films... que je montrerais pour créer ce nouveau film qui serait alors un autoportrait de moi.

Films clips are from (some films several times): *Histoires d'Amérique, D'Est, Jeanne Dielman, D'Est, Jeanne Dielman, D'Est, Hotel Monterey, D'Est, Jeanne Dielman, Lettre de cinéaste, Saute ma ville, J'ai faim, j'ai froid, Portrait d'une jeune fille, Jeanne Dielman, Saute ma ville, J'ai faim, j'ai froid, Histoires d'Amérique, Toute une nuit, Portrait d'une jeune fille, Lettre de cinéaste, Les Années 80, Golden Eighties, Un Jour Pina a demandé, Les Rendez-vous d'Anna, je tu il elle, Les Rendez-vous d'Anna, Un Jour Pina a demandé, D'Est* and *News from home.*

Sud (South)

Assistant director: Michael Garcia-Montoya.Camera: Rémon Fromont. Sound: Thierry de Halleux. Editing: Claire Atherton. Sound mix: Manna Louis, Laurent Thomas. 1999 video 16:9 colour 71'. English dialogue.

Scott MacDonald: *South* was your first American film in quite a while. What drew you to the Byrd case, in particular? It was a horrifying story.

Chantal Akerman: I read about it in a newspaper. It a very strange, terrible story. But I had wanted to make a film about the American South before the Byrd case happened.

SM: Did you start it before the Byrd case?

CA: No. But I had had the idea at the end of April, and the Byrd case happened in June – I don't remember the exact day (Byrd was murdered on June 7, 1998). I read a blurb in the newspaper, and I said, "I'm going to make the movie about the South and about what happened in Jasper, Texas." I made

plans to go to America and went to Jasper at the end of
my trip.

SM: How long after the crime did you shoot?

CA: Three months.

SM: Many of us who grew up in the 60s still have a fear of
the South.

CA: I know but, of course, that's why I went there. I had read a
book by James Baldwin – in French. I think it was called *Harlem
Quartet*; in that book Baldwin conveys so well the fear and the
silence of the South. That and the Faulkner books drove me to
do that movie.

SM: Any particular Faulkner books?

CA: I've read most of them. I mix them up. But probably *Light
in August* (1932) was important. So when the Byrd murder
happened: I said. "I have to go there," and I was lucky enough
to get to Jasper just before that memorial service in the church
because that's an incredible scene.

SM: How did you get to be present for that?

CA: I just called the minister, to have an interview with him – he
was Byrd's minister – and be said, "There's a memorial in two
days; you can come," so we went and we shot.

SM: Did anyone announce to the congregation that you were
doing the film?

CA: I don't know. But we were very welcome, as you can see.
We were totally welcome.

SM: Why are the kids hiding in the pews during the church
scene?

CA: It's part of the church ritual, I think. I don't know.

SM: Did you consider filming any of Byrd's family?

CA: No. I did not need that. I think it would have been awful
to go and say, "Hey, your father died. What do you think about
it?" – after only three months. Someone asked me how I
made decision to use any of the footage of the murder. I think
that evoking an event is usually stronger than showing news

coverage of it. But people who want to make a film about an atrocity always face the question of how much of the event to show. Claude Lanzmann found his own way in *Shoah* (1985), and other people have found their own ways. There's always a question of what to show and what not to show, and how to make people feel the event.

SM: South reminds me of several of James Benning's films, especially his *Landscape Suicide* (1986) and *Four Corners* (1997), in both the formality and length of the shots, and in the subject matter.

CA: (laughter): Well, I don't know his movies, but I know him. I met him at CalArts (Benning teaches at California Institute of the Arts in Valencia, California). He's a great guy.

SM: Also, your last shot, that almost seven-minute tracking shot down the road, along the route where Byrd was dragged, reminds me of *Shoah*.

CA: Well, as you know, one of my obsessions is the concentration camps and what happened there. But I've never seen *Shoah*: I've been afraid to see it, so I don't think Lanzmann has had any influence on me. When James Baldwin writes about the silence of the South and how he doesn't know what's hidden behind the silence. that behind the silence can be someone who wants to kill you – well, again, I was thinking of the camps.

SM: There are strange markings on that road.

CA: The marks were made by the police. That's where they found bits of Byrd's flesh and blood. The marks are fading away as the cars drive over them. We drove over them, too.

(Scott MacDonald: *A Critical Cinema: Interviews with Independent Film-makers, Volume 4*, University of California Press, 2005: 264. Thanks to Karin Tucker, University of California Press for permission to reprint.)

Akerman 20

LA CAPTIVE

BILLING

A woman's high heels clicking across Place Vendôme in
Paris. A young man (Stanislas Merhar) is following. In
Proust's *À la recherche du temps perdu*, the young woman
was Albertine, and the man Marcel. For *La Captive*, Chantal
Akerman, adapting *La prisonnière*, the fifth volume in the
series, calls the woman Ariane (Sylvie Testud) and the
man Simon.

Simon is housebound, Ariane happily not. But Simon
forces himself to follow her outside, suspecting Ariane has
girlfriends. His questions are relentless. Where has she been?
Who with?

Proust offers one kind of enquiry into such subjective agony
– though always a male one. Akerman here builds a subjectivity
for Ariane, who must negotiate surveillance and microscopic
scrutiny, at least as much she can as possible given her situation
as object, or "woman as image, man as the bearer of the look" in
Laura Mulvey's famous formulation.

In one scene of sublime cinematic invention – reminiscent
perhaps of the one of women seen in profile overlapping
another in Bergman's *Persona* – Akerman has her male
protagonist on one side of a blurred glass partition in his
bathroom, first in dialogue with the woman, then in outline
as she speaks, an unstable figure who first leans one way
and then the other in a vain attempt to merge with her body.
Simon would love to inhabit or possess Ariane's body: his
agony is boundless.

La Captive (2000, 118)'

THE HAND-OUT
Akerman 20: *La Captive*
Thursday 28 May 2015. ICA Cinema, 7pm.

La Captive

With: Stanislas Merhar, Sylvie Testud, Olivia Bonamy, Liliane Rovère, Françoise
Bertin, Aurore Clément. Screenplay: Chantal Akerman and Eric de Kuyper. Director of
photography: Sabine Lancelin. Editing: Claire Atherton. Production designer: Christian
Marti. Costume designer: Nathalie du Roscoät. Artistic director: Michel Vandestien.
Re-recording mixer: Stéphane Thiébaut. Producer: Paulo Branco. Dedicated to Jacob
Akerman. 2000 35mm 1.85: 1 colour. French with live English subtitles.

Marion Schmid: Literary adaptation, for reasons that are
easily understandable, is not a genre readily associated with
experimental or auteurist practices of film-making (despite
the fact that auteurs like Truffaut or Godard made several
films based on literary sources). Whereas commercial cinema,
mainly under the guise of the heritage genre, capitalises
on the classics of world literature which it exploits as a
lucrative foil for popular productions, the auteur tradition,
as suggested by its name, has developed largely in rivalry
with the literary medium, privileging its own scripts over a
pre-existing source text which would impose on the director
a preordained plot and aesthetic vision. Like many directors
of the post-New Wave generation, Akerman, though an avid
reader, was initially sceptical about the practice of literary
adaptation, which she considered irreconcilable with her
more purist conception of film-making and adverse to the
development of her own personal film style:

"I thought that literary works should not be adapted to film,
that music should not be used, that cuts and shots/counter-shots
should not be used — these kinds of prohibitions. I was very
radical, undoubtedly too much so, but I needed to be in order

to define myself from myself as a film-maker" (Akerman interviewed by Frédéric Bonnard, *Enthusiasm*, 4, p15)

As she reveals in an interview, she began to toy with the idea of adapting *Proust's À la recherche du temps perdu* (1913–27) back in the 1970s, more precisely after she finished *Jeanne Dielman*, yet what she herself calls her 'too dogmatic' conception of the cinema prevented her from taking the project any further at the time. It was only some twenty-five yeast later, having experimented with a wide range of genres, production modes and film styles, that she felt she had the sufficient openness and versatility required to tackle a text as complex as Proust's seven volume modernist masterpiece. Rather than taking on the whole of the *Recherche* – a project attempted by Luchino Visconti and Joseph Losey in the 1970s, but unfortunately never brought to fruition – she eventually decided to make a film loosely inspired by the fifth volume, *La Prisonnière*.

Whereas Proust's modernist style, exceptional narrative complexity and radically new conception of the self, time and space have deterred commercial directors and given his work the unjustified reputation of being unadaptable, it is precisely these aspects that were of interest to a director like Akerman, who comes from the experimental tradition *La Prisonnière* in particular, with its focus on interiority, its iterative and circular narrative structure, blurred temporality, setting in an enclosed space, and plot revolving around confinement and obsession, shares great affinities with the director's avant-garde film language and allowed her to revisit the themes of mental and spatial imprisonment that were central to films like *Jeanne Dielman*, *je tu il elle* and *L'Homme à la valise*...

The book's exploration of sexual fluidity, homosexual desire and the torments of a heterosexual relationship gave her the opportunity to continue her study of love, intimacy and desire developed in such diverse works as

Les Rendez-vous d'Anna, *Toute une nuit*, *Les Années 80* and *Golden Eighties...*"

(From Chantal Akerman, Marion Schmid, page 148, Manchester University Press 2010: 148. All rights reserved. With thanks to Marion Schmid, Matthew Frost and Manchester University Press for permission to reprint.)

Akerman 21

DE L'AUTRE CÔTÉ

BILLING

One side of the line is Arizona, the other Mexico. On one side is the town of Agua Prieta, on the other Douglas. What a difference a line makes.

The project apparently came about after Akerman read a news story on American ranchers who like to hunt clandestine immigrants with Magnum shotguns and night-vision goggles, claiming that the Mexicans were bringing dirt into America. It was this word "dirt" that struck Akerman, reminiscent as it is of the anti-Semitic vocabulary of the Nazis. The persistence of bloodlust is astonishing.

Beyond this, there are other lives and other people to talk to, not least in Agua Prieta. These faces, eyes and stories are given their time and Akerman gives them their due. We hear from the sheriff, immigration lawyers and relatives of those who didn't survive the northern passage.

Alternating with these voices, Akerman also offers wordless observation of barren, windswept roadsides or Mexicans kicking pebbles at the border wall. She gives the viewer time to reflect.

THE HAND-OUT

Akerman 21: *De l'autre côté*

Thursday 18 June 2015. ICA Cinema, 7pm.

De l'autre côté (From the Other Side)

Cameras: Chantal Akerman, Robert Fenz, Rémon Fromont. Assistant directors: Robert Fenz, Claudia Rosas Bocaro, Ricardo Padilla. Editing: Claire Atherton. Sound: Pierre Martens. Sound mix: Eric Lesachet. 2002 digital colour 1.78:1 103'. Originated on 16mm and video. French with English subtitles.

Dennis Grunes: Akerman's Mexican border towns, in colour, are parched, hazily sunlit and largely inert – the visual opposite of the border town in Orson Welles's great film noir, *Touch of Evil* (1958). Akerman portrays the towns in long shots with a fixed, level camera, creating placid scenes of dusty road and still sky. By contrast, Welles relied on angled shots, travelling shots, and closeups to get his ominous black-and-white night world right into our faces. Akerman's different vision suggests a distillation of grief, anguish and hopelessness among Mexican mourners. The little activity that we see becomes correlative to the socioeconomic doldrums, the listless poverty, that provoke illegal immigration across the border. Ironically, the hush on the Mexican side is prelude to the terrible risk on the other side and the dogging possibility of death. The tales come back of death. Theirs is a plight of desperate people who know the risk.

The vistas in Mexico are extraordinarily calm and lovely (the superb cinematographers are Rémon Fromont, Robert Fenz and Akerman) – this, a sterling example of Akerman's withering irony. Repeated shots of the seemingly endless tall, striated metal fence prohibiting Mexican flight at that point, shot at different times of day, similarly find deceptive beauty there. It's a gorgeous fence – a prettier thing, say, than the plain and practical American flag that becomes a recurrent part of Akerman's rigorous mise-en-scène. Behind this appearance, though, lurks an attitude of hostility, hatred, racism, and a casual American disregard for human life.

Throughout the film, Akerman's offscreen voice can be heard asking questions of those whom she interviews. Thus it becomes a powerful statement when, dumbfounded into silence, she listens to an American couple spouting the most sincere, awful and frightening nonsense. They speak of the gravest danger that the Mexican immigrants pose: the infliction upon the US of a smallpox epidemic. With a stupendous sense of martyrdom, the couple explain how insufficient quantities of American vaccine

will require their own sacrifice so that their grandchildren
may survive. Taking our cue from Akerman's silence, we find
the passage hilarious. (Akerman remains unseen throughout
the film.) We laugh in horror. Like everything else in the film,
however, in context the scene is tragic – for both the Mexicans,
who are dehumanised and therefore made ripe for abuse, and
the white Americans, who, by failing to embrace the humanity of
others, lose a grip on their own humanity.

Akerman has described the fear of Americans vis-à-vis the
Mexican immigrants as "[f]ear of the other, fear of his or her
poverty . . . and [of] the possibility of contagion." It is to this
that the viral epidemic that the white couple anticipate refers.
The emphasis that Arizona ranchers give to the identification of
Mexicans with "filth" suggests the fear of impurity that Akerman,
a European Jew, cannot help but identify with Nazism. In
Arizona newspapers, she found "talk of mountains of filth, as
if the filth was going to replace nature . . . [m]ountains of old
clothes, soiled diapers, plastic bottles and bags, dirty papers, etc.
There was also talk of poisoned dogs, theft, rape, and violation
of private property." Akerman has noted that, while the ranchers
feel they are in danger of losing their "lifestyle," the immigrants
are actually losing their lives."

(Dennis Grunes on his website *grunes.wordpress.com*, 2007. Dennis Grunes sadly
died on June 15, 2013. With thanks to Dennis Grunes' brother Rodney Grunes for
kind permission to reprint this review.)

MISCELLANEOUS

Babette Mangolte says that the interviews were shot on video,
with synch sound. Landscapes and general views are 16mm,
shot mute and given post-synch sound.

Akerman 22

AVEC SONIA WIEDER-ATHERTON & A L'EST AVEC SONIA WIEDER-ATHERTON

BILLING

Nothing from a film-maker as great as Akerman is ever trivial.

We believe these films have never been shown in the UK, and yet they are indelibly the work of Akerman. Music, and musical thinking, are always at the heart of Akerman's practice, and here she makes music the centre-stage subject, in homage to her friend and collaborator. But there may yet also be a reparative purpose.

Avec Sonia Wieder-Atherton (2002, 52)'
The great cellist Sonia Wieder-Atherton has been present in much of Akerman's work since the 1980s, whether on soundtracks (a great number), as a protagonist (in *Rue Mallet-Stevens*), and in this case as subject of an extended documentary showcase. In the traditional manner of French television cultural documentation, we begin with a voiceover from the film-maker, situating and describing her subject. Following this Wieder-Atherton takes over the narrative, sitting before the camera for an extended presentation of her life and art. Of particular relevance, given her relationship with Akerman, are her thoughts on interaction and exchange between artists.

Following this, Akerman moves her camera around as music is made, creating lovely views and angles and framings at will.

The music played includes a Jewish folk tune, Monteverdi, Janáĉek, Berio, Schubert, and not least Wieder-Atherton's famed partnership with the British pianist Imogen Cooper to play Brahms.

A l'est avec Sonia Wieder-Atherton, parts 1&2 (In the East with Sonia Wieder-Atherton) (2009, 44' and 42')
Sonia Wieder-Atherton announces her programme: to gather music from the east of Europe and from Mitteleuropa. First she reveals her approach to curation, to orchestration and arrangement. The composers she chooses and arranges include Rachmaninov, Dohnányi, Tcherepnin, Franck Krawczyk, Mahler and Martin. If these works have anything in common, it is above all a sense of longing, a honeyed lyricism that evokes distant horizons and resignation.

Akerman is content to find a series of angles and to edit as little as necessary, above all to limit her presence. This is a tender offering. Wieder-Atherton is a remarkable cellist. The plangent tone of the cello must bring tears to any eye. In some ways this is a recovery, or reconfiguration, of Europe as a site of culture and expression, rather than as a site of devastation, pogrom and Shoah.

THE HAND-OUT

Akerman 22: *Avec Sonia Wieder-Atherton* & *A l'est avec Sonia Wieder-Atherton*

Thursday 16 July, 2015. ICA Cinema, 6.40pm. Introduced by the producer/director/writer David Thompson.

Avec Sonia Wieder-Atherton (With Sonia Wieder-Atherton) & A l'est avec Sonia Wieder-Atherton pts 1&2 (In the East with Sonia Wieder-Atherton, parts 1 & 2)

Chantal Akerman on Sonia Wieder-Atherton: This is what we know about Sonia Wieder-Atherton.

She was born in San Francisco, grew up in New York, then Paris. She chose the cello because she wanted a string instrument with notes that she could draw out forever. Facts.

She was floored by the voices of Robeson and Callas. We know about her wrenching expressiveness, her legato. The legato she sought for years, obdurately, one-on-one with her cello. This was her goal and she fought her instrument to reach it: a vocal rapport with the music, an organic process in which each note gives birth to the next. Yes, she tried everything to make her instrument sing. To give it a voice. All of these are facts.

We know that her career path has been atypical, her repertoire, too. More vitally she is still searching, constantly going forward, looking for her own way through. To sound. Primal sound.

This, too, is true.

Sonia Wieder-Atherton on Chantal Akerman: When I think of the way Chantal Akerman films, what I see are the frames.

Each is clearly etched, creating different space.

I feel the way she looks at a scene, drawn in by the music, using the frames, their boundaries, slipping from one to the next, stopping at the edge, going round it, searching for the movement, or rather the right distance.

This, I feel, is how she creates her one-on-one dialogue. She never forces her vision upon us but simply proposes a viewpoint, almost immobile, that allows time to unfold and establish itself.

It cannot be otherwise; that time is the music.

Being filmed by Chantal is like living in the frame for the duration of the film. Even though there are moments when you want to break out and escape.

It is an image that lasts.

(With thanks to Sylviane Akerman, La Fondation Akerman, Sonia Wieder-Atherton, Pierre-Antoine Devic at Naïve Classique, and to translator Alan Fell for permission to reprint these texts.)

Avec Sonia Sonia Wieder-Atherton

Cinematography: Sabine Lancelin. Sound: Pierre-Antoine Signoret, Pierre Mertens. Production design: Christian Marti. Artistic director: Julien Azaïs. Editing: Claire

Atherton. Filmed at Château de Ferrières. Music:.Jewish prayer (arr. Jean-François Zygel). Monteverdi: *Duo Seraphim*, from *Vespro della Beata Vergine* (arr. Wieder-Atherton) Berio: *Les mots sont allés*. Janáek: *presto JW 7/6*. Brahms: *Sonata in E Minor for piano and cello, Allegro non troppo*. Monteverdi: *ritornello*, from *L'Orfeo* (arr. Wieder-Atherton. Schubert: *Litanei auf das Fest Aller Seelen*, D343. Performed by: Sonia Wieder-Atherton, cello. Imogen Cooper, piano. Sarah Iancu and Matthieu Lejeune, cellos. 2003 video colour 1.78:1 51'.

A l'est avec Sonia Wieder-Atherton – part 1

Original conception: Sonia Wieder-Atherton Cinematography: Sabine Lancelin. Sound: Pierre-Antoine Signoret. Editing: Claire Atherton. Artistic director: Anne Decoville. Set design: Christian Marti. Sound mix: Pierre-Antoine Signoret. Studio: Polish Radio, Witold Lutosławski Concert Hall. Music: Rachmaninov: *Vespers op 37, Nunc dimittis* (arr Polonsky) Dohnányi: Ruralia Hungarica op32a (arr Krawczyk) *Song in remembrance of Schubert* (Jewish trad., arr. Wieder-Atherton, Krawczyk) Tcherepnin, *Tartar danse* (orchestrated Krawczyk) Krawczyk: *jeux d'enfants, d'après les mélodies sur des poésies Moraves de Janáek*. Performed by: Sinfonia Varsovia, conducted by Christophe Mangou. Soloist: Sonia Wieder-Atherton, cello. 2008 video colour 1.78:1 43'.

A l'est avec Sonia Wieder-Atherton – part 2

Music: Kodály: *rondo Magyar* for cello and cimbalom. Prokofiev: *The Field of the Dead* from *Alexander Nevsky* score. Martinu : *variations on a Slavic theme*. Mahler: *Ich bin der Welt abhanden gekommen* (from Rückert-Lieder). *Traditional dance* (arr. Sonia Wieder-Atherton, Krawczyk). Soloists: Sonia Wieder-Atherton, cello & Cyril Dupuy, cimbalom. 2008 video colour 1.78:1 42'.

Akerman 23

DEMAIN ON DÉMÉNAGE (TOMORROW WE MOVE)

BILLING

Catherine (Clément) is recently widowed, and so moves in with her grown-up daughter Charlotte (Sylvie Testud). While Charlotte is always sympathetic, her mother brings with her the baggage of life: a grand piano, and a blustery self-centred manner that leaves Charlotte little peace and quiet for getting on with writing her pulpy, soft-core novel. Despite all, they agree to keep on living together but to look for a more spacious apartment. A raggle-taggle band of potential buyers arrive and overlap. Doors open and close and rooms get very crowded indeed, like a Feydeau farce. Charlotte has to find herself an office and gets on with writing her porn.

Akerman has often dealt with the vicissitudes of mother/daughter relationships. She has also made comedies about writer's block, about the distractions of noises off and about the appeal of rebellion in the face of insufferable constraint. A decidedly French comedic surface does not obscure Akerman's folding and unfolding of her abiding themes.

Demain on déménage (2004, 110')

THE HAND-OUT

Akerman 23: *Demain on déménage (Tomorrow We Move)*
Thursday 17 September 2015. ICA Cinema, 7.00pm.

Demain on déménage (Tomorrow We Move)

With: Sylvie Testud, Aurore Clément, Jean-Pierre Marielle, Lucas Belvaux, Dominique Reymond, Natacha Régnier, Elsa Zylberstein, Gilles Privat. Script: Chantal Akerman, Eric de Kuyper. Production designer: Christian Marti. Assistant director: Olivier Bouffar. Cinematography: Sabine Lancelin. Location sound: Pierre Mertens. Editing: Claire Atherton. Music: Sonia Wieder-Atherton. Sound mix: Thomas Gauder. 2004 35mm colour 1.66:1 110'. French with English subtitles.

Marion Schmid: From its opening sequence, *Demain on déménage* situates itself in the realm of the spectacle, the dangling instrument, as commentators have pointed out, serving as an easily decipherable metaphor for the Cinema, a spectator art par excellence whose poetry and magic, inherently dependent on technology, appear fragile and permanently threatened to the captivated viewer (Gérard Lefort, *Libération*, 3 March 2004). After a series of experimental documentaries (*Avec Sonia Wieder-Atherton*, *De l'autre côté*) made in the wake of *La Captive*, Akerman returns to fiction in sparkling form with this delightfully burlesque and energetic comedy whose choreographed mise en scène, song and dance numbers and upbeat, absurdist humour celebrate cinema's power to entertain, but also... on a deeply personal and ethical level, to pay homage to humanity's resilience arid capacity for laughter in the wake of unspeakable horror. Working once again within the parameters of a more commercially oriented production, the director gathers a prestigious cast, uniting for the first time before the camera her fetish actress Aurore Clément and her female lead from *La Captive*, the wonderfully versatile Sylvie Testud, as an endearingly dysfunctional mother-daughter couple. Jean-Pierre Marielle, one of France's most popular actors known above all for his work on stage, and young talents Natacha Régnier and Elsa Zylberstein are enlisted in supporting roles as a melancholic estate agent haunted by the Holocaust, a heavily pregnant woman who doesn't want a child, and a glamorous, upper-class wife and mother who seeks refuge from family life in a shared rented studio. Where *La Captive* had exceptionally led her to the chic west side of Paris, here the director returns to more familiar territory, multi-ethnic and socially mixed Ménilmontant, an area to the north-east of the capital where she herself has lived for several decades and which served as first abode for many Ashkenazi Jews emigrating to France in the 1920s and 1930s.

The film unravels to the rhythm of the characters' encounters in an atmosphere of joyful delirium – 'déménager' in colloquial French also means 'to lose the plot' – enhanced by Akerman's habitual principles of serialisation, accumulation and escalation. No longer bound by the strictures of realism and traditional character psychology, the narrative, flowing like an orchestral piece, develops its many narrative strands and voices, as marital and familial tensions mount and dissolve, middle-class prospective buyers tune into the contagious gaiety and chaos of the two women's bohemian existence, disaffected couples split up and new ones form in a constant coming and going across the two levels of the flat – a spatial metaphor for the Freudian unconscious according to Kaganski (Serge Kaganski, *Les Inrockuptibles*, 3 March 2004). Though not a musical in any conventional sense. Demain on déménage insistently flirts with the genre through its intermittent song-and-dance numbers, interspersed piano recitals, and the lively choreography of the actors who whirl around the cinematic space, dancing even when they are performing banal tasks like cleaning the oven or washing the sink.

Close to the work of Jacques Demy and Alain Resnais, who similarly lend enchantment to the quotidian through song and dance in their musical comedies, and to the popular operas of German composer Kurt Weill, the film also, once again, reveals Akerman's predilection for Lubitsch-style comedy and her deep affinity with Yiddish theatre and the music-hall, the two birthplaces of the burlesque."

Akerman 24

BILLING

A camera in a room. A series of shots of a window, balcony, the light of the exterior world. Offscreen we hear the voice of Akerman, on the phone. Has she been to the beach? No. She is indoors.

Akerman's camera sees life beyond, glimpses of lives lived as in Hitchcock's *Rear Window*. But the story told is very different: this is Tel Aviv, and Akerman is the daughter of Holocaust survivors. She is apprehensive about a recent bombing, and meditates on the whether Israel is indeed the 'promised land' or merely a new form of exile.

There are of course no conclusions to be drawn, because the debate is only ever at best provisional. "It's complicated," she states. Her relationship with Israel is overwhelming and frustrating, a matter of love and hate.

And what of the sea? The vast, untroubled waters have lapped these shores throughout human history. The sea is an image of freedom, or ease, of human concerns dwarfed. But as ever, it is back to the apartment, and the glimpse of a life outside, beyond the shutters.

Introduced by Nick James, editor of *Sight and Sound* magazine.

Là-bas (2006, 78')

THE HAND-OUT

Akerman 24: *Là-bas (Over There)*

Thursday 1 October 2015. ICA Cinema, 7.00pm. Introduced by Nick James, editor of *Sight & Sound* magazine.

Là-bas (Over There)

Voice, camera: Chantal Akerman. Additional camera: Robert Fenz. Editing: Claire Atherton. Sound mix: Thomas Gauder. Colour grading: Vonnick Guénée. Producers: Marilyn Watelet, Elizabeth Gérard. 2006 video colour 1.78:1 78' French and English, with subtitles.

Q: Why make this film?

Chantal Akerman: Basically, I didn't want to at all. I have never wanted to make a film in Israel. It was Xavier Carniaux, who produces most of my documentaries, who suggested it to me one day. My immediate feeling was that it was a bad idea, even an impossible idea – almost paralysing and downright repulsive. I don't understand any of that, he told me. You're the one person who I would hope to make such a film. I answered that I didn't want it and that people shouldn't expect anything from me. I understood quite well why he made this suggestion to me in particular, but it was all much too obvious – Israel and me, Chantal Akerman. I expressed my reluctance and my scruples. I was afraid I would burn my fingers and my reason. I was afraid my subjectivity was an obstacle, dangerous, and confused in relation to this theme. There is no neutrality; it could only be feigned. When I make a documentary, my greatest desire is that it has nothing directly to do with my own story or that of the Jews. And if it does, as in *Histoires d'Amérique*: Food, Family and Philosophy, then I stage it as thoroughly as for the theatre, so that a distance arises – and this distance makes everything possible. But when I make a film like *Sud (South)*, for example, in which I call into memory the stillness, the fear, and the lynching of blacks, at the same time I also invoke another stillness that, for me, is the stillness of the camps or over the camps, the loud stillness in the kitchen – but not

explicitly... But I thought that, to contemplate Israel, one had
to go to Afghanistan, or somewhere else, like New York, but
certainly not Israel... Then, when I went to Tel Aviv University
to teach film, I told Xavier I would take my camera along and
we'd see... In Israel, I began reading again and taking notes, and
then it happened. Just a few metres from where I lived, during
a declared truce in March or February, 2005, I don't remember.
But the attack in the immediate vicinity of where I lived was not
the decisive thing. Decisive was that one day I took the camera
and sat down somewhere and suddenly there was an image, a
shot. I thought it was a great picture. After that, all I had to do
was wait and let things run their course.

Q: But not just a shot, this was a whole film...?

CA: Yes, but I didn't know that yet. I began with a shot.

Q: Indeed, this is an incarnation, which is so resonant, so
meaningful. Why is it so difficult to leave this place?

CA: For me it is. That's how I feel everywhere, by the way. Here
as much as down there. I looked out of the window, which
was hidden by bamboo shades with very narrow slats and very
narrow spaces between them. I could see through them, but
not be seen myself – at least that's what I think. It was like in
front of a stage.

Q: So you were concealing yourself in order to observe? It's
impossible not to think of Anne Frank behind her shutter,
looking for a glimpse of life in Amsterdam...

CA: ... For me it is always a heroic act to go outside. In this case
especially, maybe also because of the film I was supposed to
make and that I suspected would happen elsewhere, namely
outside... Almost all the windows were closed, almost all the
blinds were rolled down except at the window to the terrace –
an opening with bright light.

Q: You said just now 'down there'. Where is that? Israel maybe?

CA: A relationship to here, to Paris, to Europe arises there. Yes,
"down there" is Israel. Israel ought to be the end of exile, it

ought to be about making recuperation – but it isn't always, not even in imagination. I don't believe it is. So I speak of an inner prison, the way one speaks of an illness. People die and commit suicide in Israel, too. There is no paradise.

Q: So *Là-bas* can be seen as a film about how film looks and sees…?

CA: Basically, yes. The film gives the viewer lots of space. The viewer is beside me in the apartment.

Q: The apartment is a kind of cinema auditorium?

CA: Yes. And vice versa.

Q: So this is a film about film? The viewer is an active participant, alone with the shot, the view of the blinds, with those people, that street. Free, one might say. While you are not, you are incarnated. The viewer by contrast is given an absolute freedom perhaps?

CA: Yes, I hope so.

Q: Which is to offer a different experience of film, something like an art installation, yet not that, it is undeniably a film. Is there a relationship to *Rear Window*?

CA: Yes, but in *Rear Window* there is the direct reverse shot of James Stewart, to mediate between his viewpoint and the viewer. Here the viewer is the reverse shot. That way I avoid idolatry and doubtless also the excessive pleasure that cinema can be.

(From an interview, conducted by Franck Nouchi, Paris, January 2006. With thanks to Sylviane Akerman and La Fondation Akerman to reprint Akerman's words. The questions have been paraphrased freely as Franck Nouchi could not be contacted.)

Akerman 25

LA FOLIE ALMAYER

BILLING

Chantal Akerman's final foray into fictional film-making, her very free adaptation of Joseph Conrad's tale of colonial ennui.

Almayer is not a well man. His house has seen better times and the jungle aims to take it back. His Malaysian wife is mad. Their daughter has been sent away for a better life and an education.

This is Conrad's novel about the malaise of a prospector in the dog days of colonialism. Conrad would have his protagonist forget, forget his wife and daughter, and die happy. Akerman, as we might expect, allows her Almayer no such comfort. He will see the horror of it all and die in agony.

Almayer's Folly is Akerman's dramatic swansong, a final statement of her imagined worlds. The metaphoric image of a film-maker sitting amid the ruin of cinema is inescapable.

Introduced by Gregor Muir, Director of the Institute of Contemporary Arts, and by film editor Claire Atherton who first worked with Chantal Akerman on *Letters Home*, the start of a long-standing collaboration on Akerman's fiction films, documentaries and installations.

La Folie Almayer (2011, 127')

BLOG

On Chantal Akerman

ICA Bulletin, 19 October 2015. See page 213.

THE HAND-OUT

Akerman 25: *La Folie Almayer*

22 October 2015. ICA Cinema, 7pm.

This screening is dedicated to the memory of
Chantal Akerman
6 June 1950 – 5 October 2015

Introduced by Gregor Muir, Director of the Institute of
Contemporary Arts, and by film editor Claire Atherton who
first worked with Chantal Akerman on *Letters Home*, the start
of a long-standing collaboration on Akerman's fiction films,
documentaries and installations.

La Folie Almayer

Cinematography: Rémon Fromont. Editing: Claire Atherton. Production design:
Patrick Dechesne, Alain-Pascal Housiaux. Sound: Pierre Martens, Cécile Chagnaud,
Thomas Gauder Colourist: Peter Bernaers. Cast: Stanislas Merhar, Aurora Marion,
Marc Barbé, Zac Andrianasolo, Sakhna Oum, Solida Chan, Yucheng Sun, Bunthang
Khim. 2011 35mm DCP colour 1.85:1 127'. French with English subtitles.

Eva-Lynn Jagoe: (Spoiler alert) He had a fixed idea that if he
should not forget before he died he would remember to all
eternity," writes Conrad. "Certain things had to be taken life,
stamped out of sight, destroyed, forgotten." The last pages
of the novel narrate this implacable determination, and in
the end Almayer is found dead with a calm look on his face,
showing that he "had been permitted to forget before he died."
Chantal Akerman's *La Folie Almayer* is not so kind: in its final,
unbroken, minutes-long shot, it considers the ravaged face
of Almayer (Stanislas Merhar) as he is forced to confront his
folly, to face it in all its unrelenting horror. The extraordinary
opacity of this final shot is inversely related to the
psychological cataclysm taking place within Almayer's mind,
his annihilating rush of self-knowledge depicted not through

(conventional) drama but duration – thus remaining, in a crucial dimension, unreadable, unknowable to the audience. Yet it is this very tension between knowing and not knowing that gives this final shot its remarkable, wrenching power: a painful plenitude that evokes physically, phenomenologically, the self-annihilating folly/delusion to which Almayer has willingly yielded.

Folly (from the French 'fou') is something which goes beyond a fault or flaw. It is something that one falls prey to, stoops to, gives in to; a madness that consumes the whole being. Unlike Conrad, Akerman does not make this madness a property of Almayer's (la folie de Almayer), but rather conjoins it with his being; she gives the madness a name and a face. Each madness has a specificity which renders it unique; each madness is one's own, particular to the coordinates and disorientations of oneself. That self is, of course, an inherited one, formed through the biological and cultural memories and experiences that shape it, and thus *La Folie Almayer* is not one that resides solely in Almayer, but in the child he haplessly, helplessly consigns to a life between two worlds.

Akerman evokes the lineal descent of this madness through a circular structure. In the opening sequence, a listless karaoke performance is interrupted by sudden violence: the young man lip-synching on stage is stabbed by an assailant and pulled out of the frame by onlookers, while his backup dancers scatter, leaving a single girl still dancing vacantly to the canned music. "Nina – he's dead," an offscreen voice utters; and as the news gradually seems to sink in, the camera moves in to a close shot of the girl we do not yet know as Almayer's daughter as she begins to sing, hesitantly and then intensely, a religious song in Latin. The studied obliqueness immediately invites our questions: Why is this dark-skinned woman singing a Christian hymn in archaic European Latin? What does her mounting euphoria signify? Release and relief at the brutal end of an abusive relationship, an unlikely salvation, or an irretrievable descent into madness?

"The questions posed at the beginning have not been answered by the time of the mirrored final shot, though the lineaments of the muted narrative have given them some context. Almayer has resided at his forsaken outpost for a number of years at the urging of the entrepreneur and explorer Lingard (Marc Barbé), who has promised him wealth and urges him to think of himself as a cultured European – even as he coerces the deluded trader into a loveless marriage with his ward, a Malaysian woman who stubbornly rejects the language and culture that is forced upon her. Nina is the outcome of this undesired union, and for Almayer his one raison d'être apart from the illusory bonds of race and class. When Lingard – who, it would seem, orchestrates all aspects of Almayer's life – insists that Nina must be sent to a European boarding school, Almayer begs his "benefactor" to let her remain, saying that he loves her and she him, that she is all he has in this uncivilised jungle. Lingard is adamant, and essentially challenges Almayer to prove his faith in the future that he has been promised. Like Abraham sacrificing Isaac, Almayer submits, demonstrating his unwavering fidelity to the religion of profit, white superiority, and culture that Lingard preaches.

(From a review by Eva-Lynn Jagoe, *Cinema Scope CS49*, Dec 2011. With thanks to Eva-Lynn Jagoe and to Andrew Tracy at Cinema Scope for permission to reprint this text.)

MISCELLANEOUS

Claire Atherton's introductory address:
First of all I would like to tell you Sylviane's own words about Chantal.

"My sister had a sickness, called manic depression. It is this sickness which is the cause of her death. I can't explain anything more. And anyway there is nothing to explain. She is not here anymore, and that's all. And she has said everything in her œuvre, in her work."

I remember when Chantal came here to meet Joanna and Adam the first time. It was during the editing of *No Home Movie*, last year in May. When she came back to Paris she told me how much she was happy to have met them, and that they were doing beautiful work. I know she came a few times after that, to present her films here. And she was overwhelmed by the audience's reception to her and her work.

Chantal was a very tender person. And I have the feeling I see this tenderness in the eyes of the ones who loved her. When we were editing *La Captive*, I was going to take her every morning at her home, and we would drive to Les Studios de Joinville. Each morning she would say either, "the sky is grey like a mouse," or, "the sky is blue tender." And then she would say "I have to call my mother," and she would call her mother in the car.

Chantal was very funny, too. And sometimes a little clumsy. I would like to make you laugh a little bit tonight because I think she would have loved that. So I will tell you a little story about my shirt. This afternoon I spilled some tea on my blue shirt. It was my blue shirt she liked so much. She used to spill things on her shirts right before important rendez-vous. So maybe I did it to make her laugh?

I would like to add that Chantal loved Stanislas Merhar very deeply…

(With thanks to Claire Atherton for permission to reprint this text.)

Akerman 26

NO HOME MOVIE

BILLING

(Note: this billing was prepared prior to news of Akerman's death)

Akerman's latest film is her most heartfelt piece of film-making to date. Akerman's work so often dwells on the mother and daughter relationship, on dependence, on separation, longing and loss. In *No Home Movie*, Akerman places her mother centre-stage, her camera recording the utter devotion of one for the other. This relationship has formed Akerman, sustaining her through a lifetime of wandering, in aesthetically remote regions.

The film opens with a shot of a leafless desert tree, bowed by an endless wind. Meanings blossom on this tree as only a flower in the desert can do: profusely, astonishingly, pathetically.

No Home Movie

With: Natalia Akerman, Sylviane Akerman, Chantal Akerman. Camera/sound: Chantal Akerman. Editing: Claire Atherton. Sound mix: Eric Lesachet. Picture grading: Peter Bernaers. Produced by: Patrick Quinet, Serge Zeitoun, Chantal Akerman. 2015 digital video colour 1.78:1 113'. 30 October 2015 Regent Street Cinema, 7.30pm.

THE HAND-OUT

No hand-out was prepared.

MISCELLANEOUS

This screening was planned to coincide with the opening of the exhibition at Ambika P3 Gallery, curated by *A Nos Amours* and Michael Mazière for Ambika P3. News of Akerman's death meant that this screening became a posthumous screening. Joanna

Hogg, Adam Roberts and Claire Atherton introduced the film,
a film to close the retrospective. In this way, the retrospective
unexpectedly and sadly became a complete survey of Akerman's
body of work for the cinema.

Claire Atherton's address

I know Chantal would have been happy to see you all here. I
even think she is somehow here with us. I have been in London
for two weeks now, working with Joanna, Adam, Michael,
Carole, Christoph, Jesse, Mo, Heather, Niall and many others,
to the preparation of the exhibition in P3. And we all had the
feeling she was with us, helping us to take the right decisions, to
be confident.

Chantal was a very intuitive person. She had the capacity to
listen and trust her intuition, and she knew it would lead her,
it would lead us, somewhere. With Chantal, each film, each
installation, was a discovery, was like a 'first time'. She was not
following any rules or any principle. Nothing was forbidden
for her. She didn't like to explain her choices, she didn't like to
give reasons, because her work is always questioning and not
answering. And that is what makes it strong and alive.

As I said last Thursday, the first time she came in London to
see the Ambika P3 exhibition space was in May 2014, and it was
during the editing of *No Home Movie*. I remember when she
came back she was very excited to have met Joanna, Adam and
Michael. And she told me: "the space is incredible ! I will tell you
more tomorrow… Now, let's work."

The first title of *No Home Movie* was *Home Movie*. Chantal
wanted to say with this title that it was a home-made movie,
filmed entirely by herself (some of the footage she had even
forgotten) and edited in her home. And also a film about home.
But someone told us that *Home Movie* sounded a little bit like
home cinema. And so, she said, "Oh, so it will be
No Home Movie. It's even stronger. Because I don't belong

to any home…" That was the way Chantal was thinking. Deep and quick.

When the film was showed in Locarno, Chantal went on the stage before the screening and said, "It's a film about loss."

I would just like to add that Sylviane Akerman, Chantal's sister, is here with us tonight.

(With thanks to Claire Atherton for permission to reprint this text.)

Blogging

BY ADAM ROBERTS

In defence of Akerman's *L'Enfant aimé*

(In support of Akerman 1, posted to *ICA Bulletin*, 27 November 2013.)

L'Enfant aimé – ou je joue à être une femme mariée (1971)
will be screened in the opening programme of a complete
retrospective of Chantal Akerman's film work. This screening
of *L'Enfant aimé* is presented for the first time with English
subtitles. It is a very rarely seen film. Indeed, the film has been
disparaged by Akerman herself, and so has been little discussed
by commentators, but it arguably opens up a project that finds
fulfilment in later work.

A Nos Amours begin exploration of Akerman's film work with
her first three shorts – *Saute ma ville*, *L'Enfant aimé* and *Hotel
Monterey*. While her first and third films have been admired
and much written about, *L'Enfant aimé*, her second, has not.
And yet, looking at this film, noting that it is the film she made
almost immediately after the Pierrot le fou-like antics of *Saute
ma ville*, *L'Enfant aimé* seems an odd, immediate departure for
Akerman from the stylistics of that first film, a departure that I
say anticipates in several remarkable ways the work for which
she is celebrated.

Akerman's initial dismissal of *L'Enfant aimé* was made
while talking of her encounter with Jonas Mekas in New York.
Akerman records his approval of *Saute ma ville* (he called it her
'Chaplin film'), but evidently he did not approve of her second.
Akerman's reasoning in regard to *L'Enfant aimé* is obscure - she
made an annotated filmography for Nicole Brenez, marking it
simply: "A failure, lost."

Incidentally, Akerman has recently shown a part of the film as an installation work – a scene where a woman (the 'young mother') stands in front of a mirror and submits herself to self-scrutiny, naming bodyparts, evaluating bodyparts and making some critical assessment of herself. There is repetition and circularity in the naming and wording. This stand-alone use of the scene does not include the visible presence of Akerman herself, which is such an important part of the full films. This re-use, in 2007, was titled *In the Mirror*, screened from DVD, and ran at 14'32".

Her third film (*Hotel Monterey*), as she has often said, was made following Akerman's encounter with the work of Michael Snow and Andy Warhol. *Hotel Monterey* is a mute series of shots inside and on the roof of a hotel in New York. It is a serene and poised affair, made according to strict structural principles. *L'Enfant aimé* stands apart from that film too, being in some ways narrative, including dialogue and scene-setting, thus pointing ahead to *Le 15/8*, the film she would make on her return to Europe, and beyond that to *Jeanne Dielman*.

By the way, the fact that the kitchen locale of *Saute ma ville* is strikingly similar to the kitchen seen in *Jeanne Dielman* is, to me, a red herring.

Given that *L'Enfant aimé – ou je joue à être une femme mariée* has been so little seen, it seems wise to begin with some description of the film.

To begin with, *L'Enfant aimé* is shot b&w, with location sound recording of very variable quality and audibility. I don't think this is a mistake, I think it is a material condition of the work, and serves interesting ends. The voice of the woman (the 'young mother', played by Claire Wauthion) that Akerman in this film spends time with (visibly so), is more or less audible, either because of the positioning of a microphone, or because of the background noise that sometimes drowns her out. This, I take to be a decision because it is consistent with the approach

to geography of the domestic space: exterior spaces (such as
terraces, or backyards), outside of the strict confine of 'home',
are situations where there is marked reduction of the clarity –
we can't hear well and conversation is desultory and unclear.
Outside, all is noise, din and confusion. Inside all is calm and
voices audible. Purity and clarity (of course) are not necessarily
virtues; mess can be a form of expression or resistance. The
geography, the relationship of the spaces, how the doors and
corridors are laid out, is not easily envisaged, as in *Jeanne
Dielman*. It would take some work to produce a ground plan.

Strikingly Akerman herself is often in the frame, not as a
performer, as in *Saute ma ville*, and not as behind the camera
auteur, chooser of shots and framings, as in *Hotel Monterey*, but
fully in the shot, attending closely to her friend's talk and daily
life. She is a curious presence: not participating in the scene,
but nevertheless there before us. Akerman's presence changes
the nature of the gaze, dislocating the metaphysics and politics
of looking. She is not in every shot, but she is so often there
that even when she is not there, she is there by implication.
The pattern of her presence and absence is structured, for me,
in an analogous way to interior/exterior: Akerman's presence
provokes the young mother's reflective remarks; when absent,
the young mother becomes full of purpose, action and then
overt expression of thoughts – albeit that she seems often driven
by anxiety, with a tendency to repetition and circularity. For
example, when Akerman is there, the conditions of married
life can be talked of, calmly and dispassionately, but when
she is absent, the woman's own body becomes the focus of
examination, description and a listing of merits and demerits (as
in the mirror sequence mentioned above). Clothes and outfits
are tried out.

Akerman being present in frame means that when she is not
there, we are nevertheless very much aware that she might be so
at any moment.

The child of the title may not be the child we see in the film. Yes, that child is beloved (how tenderly she is treated!), but there are other senses of 'child' that spring to mind when watching this film. That the two women have been children themselves came to my mind: there is a tangible sense of play, of dressing up, of regarding one's own body – in the way that children do – noticing change, noticing the individuality of a body, as if change had just been noticed. The relationship of the women suggested to me a sense of sisterly intimacy (I am avoiding the thought that they might be lovers, since the young mother talks constantly about her absent husband, and their sexual life together).

The sense that time is passing, sometimes slowly, sometimes as if there is not enough of it (the pacing changes sharply several times) is inescapable throughout the film. If toys must be tidied away, we see all of that task; if a window must be shut, we see all of the journey to that room and that action; if dinner must be cooked, we are not spared the washing-up.

Akerman's patient observation of detail, of the flurries of activity without obvious cause, and the confusion in my mind about the geography of the apartment, suggests to me that for that young mother control and mastery of an environment are not possible. It would seem that the adult woman is not at ease in herself – perhaps in the way a girl-child self-consciously plays at mother, wife, householder. The performance of being a woman, so poignant when attempted by a child, is no less so when undertaken by an adult woman - the isolation of days spent waiting for a husband, of attempting to come to terms with the decline of first love, of the realisation that the husband is in need of "mothering", or the limits of sexual pleasure in this situation. For this condition, the condition of 'young mother', in that place, in that life, all that can be worked with is pace. And love of a child.

There are no men here. Men are talked of, never seen. The
man's clothes are of course touched and tidied – the objects
given reverential handling. In the absence of the man, the tactile
quality of fabric is a thing in itself.

Akerman onscreen listens. Does she listen for herself, for
us, or for the women she listens to? That she is sometimes
close enough to her friend to hear clearly, when we the film
audience cannot quite hear what is being said, is interesting.
Moreover, Akerman is presumably privy to her friend's life
and situation outside the film. Importantly, Akerman does not
respond. She is attentive, but she does not (as people who talk
often do) mirror her friends physical attitudes or emotional
outpourings. Her listening is a remarkable feat – active
always, never passive and never indifferently. Her lively bodily
movements as she follows or adjusts herself to better hear and
better attend is part of the mystery and formal invention of this
film. I know of no precedent.

The sound work is percussive. The heels of the woman drum
on the parquet flooring, doors shut hard, furniture is dragged
without thinking of the neighbours, cooking implements are
used noisily. The sounds are orchestrated, laid out as if in a
score. The sound levels in compressed 16mm optical sound
are generally unmerciful and without subtlety. Sounds are
placed, not adjusted. The pattern of the edit is mirrored by the
patterning of the sound world. This is a constructed edifice –
no less so than a brutalist building. The interiors are all hard
surfaces and the location sound recording cannot disguise the
sharp reverberations of the sound world. This is how enclosure,
interiority, confinement sounds. The habitual life of meal
times, of cleaning, of putting things into order, has this very
soundtrack. Anyone who has lived it knows it; anyone who
hasn't will feel like they always did.

What is narrated? Ostensibly, the woman and her child live an
ordered life, and that is the narrative. The child must be cared

for, the cooking, cleaning, and making all ready for the return of
her husband have to be done, and in good time.

The 'young mother' talks of her sex life, of the diminishing
of her married sex life, of the childish emotional needs of
her husband ("he's such a baby!"). She talks of her sense of
confinement, and yet when she is out on her errands she meets
no one and talks to no one. She is in control of the openings to
her home: the window can be closed, the exterior and interior
doors shut and locked, stuff can be put away tidily, objects may
be rearranged.

What of the mirror in her bedroom? This is, naturally, a
thing that reflects, not the reflection that comes from talking
with another (her friend Chantal, for example), but a means
to examine the image of herself at play with her daughter, of
herself trying out various outfits, in various combinations, or
without clothes subjecting herself to a critique. If there is to
be thought, a mirror helps, at least in order to make possible
reflexivity: this is me, pointing at the other.

These are the material conditions of this film, and so much
of it seem so arresting, so eloquent. This is no failure, but a
moment of creation of strategies that have no precedent.

I would like to emphasise the percussive sound world,
the deliberate obfuscation of the internal geography of the
apartment, the compartmentalisation of life lived in rooms,
each with specific kinds of activity reserved for them, the careful
opening and closing of doors that serve as valves between these
rooms, and variation of bodily pace and movement as if anxiety
must from time to time be eluded.

Le 15/8 is another rarely seen film. In it, Akerman presents
a stream-of-consciousness in voiceover, that of a young
Danish woman in Paris. She is there looking for work, in an
apartment that is not her own. Time passes, and her thoughts
are heard, in seamless flow, evoking for some the world of
Woolf's *Mrs Dalloway*. But in *Le 15/8*, there is no party to

prepare for: instead the contents of a handbag are the subject of her preoccupation, or if not that then any number of other commonplaces. There is also ceaseless critical judgments, a constant need to take issue with one' own body. But this, presented in voiceover, means that the locus of criticism lies outside herself, that seems to me to emerge directly from the mirror sequence of *L'Enfant aimé*.

What *Le 15/8* and *Jeanne Dielman* also share with *L'Enfant aimé* is above all a sense of domestic spaces presented as a series of interconnected ventricles, in which life is represented as a rhythmical process, with the pulse, form and function of each of the parts made very clear. Function and physical limit define the possibilities of life, this all too recognisable form of constrained life. It must be lived as best it can.

We can only hope that *L'Enfant aimé – ou je joue à être une femme mariée* will enjoy restoration and further screenings and other eyes.

Preparing to see *Jeanne Dielman...*
(In support of Akerman 3, posted on *ICA Bulletin*, 10 December 2013.)

How best to approach a screening of *Jeanne Dielman, 23 Quai du Commerce, 1080 Bruxelles*? If you have seen it before, you will know that it runs at 201 minutes, or 3 hours and 21 minutes. You will know that it tells of a middle-aged woman living in a one-bedroom apartment in Brussels, with her schoolboy son. Every day he is duly packed off to school, while household matters must be addressed prior to an afternoon call from men who pay for sex. That should not be too much of a spoiler, since the plot is well enough known, and the film dates from 1975.

The most arresting aspect of this film is of course the fact that everything happens in what could be called real time. A potato

takes just as long to peel onscreen as it does in real life. There
is relatively little by way of the familiar compression of action or
editing out of what a mainstream entertainment would regard
as irrelevant. The action, moreover, takes place for the most
part in a small apartment, but nevertheless an apartment that
offers ample opportunity for movement and drama: so many
doors to open and close, so many lights to switch on and off,
so many objects to move from here to there and there to here.
The surfaces being hard, reflect and sustain the sharpness of the
sounds that heels make on the uncarpeted floors, water running
for the washing up, that pans make on stove tops, and so on.

But there is domestic calm here, too: a comfortable parlour,
that doubles as the son's bedroom, the sofa exploding out to
become a bed. And the money that makes all this possible, that
pays for the food and the rent, that the gentlemen pay Mdme
Dielman as they take their leave each afternoon, is kept in a Delft
tureen, placed in the centre of the dining table, a centrepiece
for the apartment and these lives. The son knows that if he asks
nicely he will be given a little extra from the tureen.

That Delft tureen might bring to mind the painting of the
Low Countries. The tureen is the product of industry meeting
bourgeois appetites. It permits the elegant presentation of soup,
the daily staple that Jeanne provides her son. And the painters
of the Low Countries that emerged to portray the bourgeois and
petit bourgeois lives in an astonishing departure from sacred
themes, did so with some affection. They loved doorways as
framing devices, not as keyholes, but as markers of the domestic
interior, of comfortable private domains. Thresholds are tender
transitions from an exterior that may be impersonal to an
interior that is always personal.

And so it is for Jeanne – her excursions require her to be well
prepared – lipstick, hair spray, coiffure – all as they should be.
Comme il faut. Her preparations for the arrival of the gentleman
callers of course require a similar level of personal attention

– the mirrors in this apartment are employed only when an encounter with another is anticipated. They reflect what the outside world will see. In the privacy of the domestic world there is no need for that anxiety. The domestic space is not, if regarded in this light, always a prison, as is easy to assume.

Averted gaze is another characteristic of *Jeanne Dielman*. Eyes do not meet, eyelines do not connect, there are no reverse angles to suggest anything of that kind of interaction. This is a drastic radicalism in cinema. Akerman herself was very ready to meet the camera's gaze in *La Chambre* but here Jeanne is often shot square, framed geometrically, without camera movement to adjust to bodily movement. Jeanne inhabits this frame and does not much seek to leave it. If Jeanne meets another while out and about, her eyes are likely to look down, and if she shares a meal with her son, they sit at right angles to each other. Even when the boy is in bed and Jeanne takes her leave of him, by clever contrivance, they are never face to face as they kiss goodnight.

This avoidance is a marker of the radicalism of New York – where Akerman soaked up the experimental film-making at Anthology Film Archives, a few blocks away from Judson Church, where Yvonne Rainer and others had been pursuing a radical dance agenda. In Rainer's 1969 statement given out for *The Mind is a Muscle* show:

"It is my overall concern to reveal people as they are engaged in various kinds of activities – alone, with each other, with objects – and to weigh the quality of the human body towards that of objects and away from the super-stylization of the dancer."

Moreover, as she has said of her *Trio A*:

"Two primary characteristics of the dance are its unmodulated continuity and its imperative involving the gaze. The eyes are always averted from direct confrontation with the audience via independent movement of the head or closure of the eyes or simple casting down of the gaze."

The energy of these enquiries has, it might seem, readily infused itself into the strategies and design of *Jeanne Dielman*. The delight of this film for me is very much about the discovery of a form of cinema that brings the radicalism of New York into fruitful union with the framed domestic interiors of the Low Countries.

I detect three pivotal moments.

The first is a moment about what is not said, about what does not happen. The son reads his classroom exercise, a poem by Baudelaire, *The Enemy*. It is a poem about the need in later life to foster some sense of order so that there can be a fruitful denial of death. No mention of this sentiment, rather talk of the quality of the boys pronouncing of 'r' sounds (important in Belgium where French vies with Flemish).

Following this, a sentimental ballad plays on the radio. It distracts Jeanne from her dutiful writing of a letter. The son knows that it has intruded on his mother's peace of mind. It has, but Jeanne makes sure they stick to the routine, and the evening constitutional means that the radio is switched off. If only I knew what the song was exactly (please post a comment if you know!).

After this comes an outburst, which for those who have not seen the film, will be described simply as an astonishing and perplexing dialogue between mother and son at bedtime.

All else follows from these moments: the first a question of denial, the second a question of perturbation without explanation, the third the beginning of the end.

The film has been much analysed, and analysed brilliantly, but the merit of repeat viewing is a developing awareness of furniture, objects, the pattern of the chores that varies microscopically, revealingly. One grows aware of 'the quality of the human body towards that of objects and away from… super-stylization'.

Finally, Akerman has talked (an interview in *Camera Obscura* in 1977) of the fact that it was her own adoring observation of her own mother's movements and activities in her home, in her private domestic domain, that informed and shaped *Jeanne Dielman*. The love of her mother certainly emerges for me in this superb and compassionate characterisation, that sidesteps cliché, that brings a genuine radical purpose into perfect realisation, and that (as Ezra Pound might have said) is news that stays news.

Planning a screening: *News from home*

(In support of Akerman 4, posted on *ICA Bulletin*, 21 January 2014.)

Akerman made two versions – one in English and one in French – which should perhaps not surprise us since she, more than many film artists, has one foot in the New York of Michael Snow, Jonas Mekas and Andy Warhol, and the other in the Europe of André Delvaux, Jean-Luc Godard and Rainer Werner Fassbinder (all mentioned and discussed by Akerman at various times).

These two versions of this film offer identical images and sound atmospherics, but differ in that Akerman's voice reads letters from her mother in one case in French, and the other in English. Delivery and tone differ somewhat – in French, Akerman is speaking in her native language, the language she shares with her mother, and in the English, an acquired language after all, and one that her mother may or may not know.

These letters were written and first read when Akerman was in New York in 1972, a stay that produced *Hotel Monterey* and *La Chambre*. Of course the English-language version is a translation – no credit is given for translation, but this was done presumably by Akerman herself. This is a further point of difference then: the English-language version offers words not just selected and edited by a daughter, but have passed into and through, in the act of translation, a daughter.

The French version comes across as perhaps more casually read, more easily read, less formal. The English version, given the relative unfamiliarity of the language, seems perhaps more affirmative, more declamatory. Ackerman has described her voiceover as intended as a kind of psalmody, a murmured incantation. To hear both versions will be a chance to compare and contrast.

When planning this screening, we found that we could book a 16mm print with the French soundtrack, without subtitles, which is how the film has necessarily most often been seen. Luckily, the Royal Belgian Film Archive have digitised *News from home*, and could offer us the English-language version.

We wondered what to do. If we wish to present the film (as is our habit) in original format (in this case 16mm film) should we then attempt to project subtitles, cued live, with dirt and scratches and joins? Or should we screen the restored film, as so many back catalogue films now are, cleaned of 'defects', and with the rare English-language soundtrack?

Of course watching subtitled films is a deeply familiar experience for most of us. We watch films hardly noticing our eyes flicking up and down, reading the lines, then seeing speakers move their lips to make utterances in a language we speak badly or not at all. But then by some mysterious alchemy we start to hear them speak in English (I'm assuming you, like me, to be a native English speaker).

The rhythm of the titles coming and going soon fades from awareness. I suggest that we hardly notice the dynamic edge that this procedure adds to our experience of a film.

I am not suggesting that subtitling is ever a mistake. Dubbing in some parts of the world is the norm – where a few actors re-record the lines and that is used to make a new soundtrack in the local language. In Italy, the actors whose voices are familiar because they have dubbed so many films are themselves celebrities. Dubbing is of course a kind of remaking of a film, surely always more radical than subtitling. And bedevilling both approaches is the problem of translation – always faulty and often just plain wrong.

To return to the screening of *News from home*, and its possible subtitling. The coming and going of subtitles is not nothing – it is a very profound intrusion into the intended rhythms of a film work. In the case of a work of such gentle and surreptitious rhythmical structuring as *News from home*, subtitles would perhaps be an utterly destructive intrusion. I watched the film again and found myself reading and not looking, and only then when the flow of subtitles halts for a while, having the chance to look and stare at the images. When the flow of subtitles resumed my attention scuttled back to them, leaving me anxious in case I had missed a few. Not so good.

For these reasons, Joanna and I wondered about a double bill screening, first of the English-language version of *News from home*, so that we might first take in what it is that is being said, and then with the restored French-language version without subtitles, be in a position to take in the film itself as the sole source of rhythm.

This will divide the audience of course – some will speak French, while others will not. We will, by the way, make available paper copies of the text in English to anyone who wants it.

Other concerns to consider: the restored copy lacks 'weave', that gentle movement of the frame due to camera and projector imperfections, and the restored copy has clean sound, without the analogue hiss and limited frequency range of a 16mm film optical soundtrack. The film copy has colour faded (it has 'magenta lift'), it has joins and dirt and scratches. The restored copy looks like it was shot yesterday. The film copy looks like an archaeological relic – it looks its age.

We are also interested in the experience of watching this film twice in quick succession (forgetting the language difference for now). This is a rare way of seeing films nowadays, though once upon a time it was possible to sit through successive

programmes in cinemas, whereas nowadays the auditorium is
cleared between screenings.

In any case, it was certainly rare for us to watch a film again
straight away, until we began running films and prints to
check their condition shortly before screening them with an
audience. These repeat viewings have been a revelation. The
films have seemed to us to be positively enhanced by this repeat
encounter. This goes for the films we knew well, films we had
seen long ago, or films we had never before seen.

Chantal Akerman's films in particular have certainly benefited
from the chance to see them repeatedly. Repeat viewings
show her films to be endlessly surprising, and despite use of
repetition and often minimal staging, full of rich and rewarding
detail that we might otherwise have missed. This is true even
(perhaps especially so) of *Jeanne Dielman*, which runs of
course for more than three hours. One viewing might reveal
details of movement and choreography, another of structuring,
and another sound design. Each viewing reveals something new.

For us, repeat viewings have made the films more visible,
more gripping, more admirable. We wonder what you will think.

On Chantal Akerman's *Les Rendez-vous d'Anna*

(In support of Akerman 5, posted on *ICA Bulletin*, 12 February 2014.)

Akerman's protagonists in *Les Rendez-vous d'Anna* move as if
without plans. A phone call or a message picked up in hotel lobby
can cause a sudden change of itinerary. Does a train go to Cologne?
– well, if so, then why not? Plans are made to take a room at a hotel
on the spur of the moment. Lovemaking is suspended even after
looked forward to with relish a moment before. Only the voice
of a man with instructions for a trip yet to be taken on an answer
machine seems certain about what is to happen next, but then we
suspect such expectations are entirely provisional.

It is hard not to think that all is exhaustion, all ennui. Passion is spent, ardour absent, partings taken without the comfort of contact, no hugs, no kisses. Regret has to be inferred. Often a jump cut elides a moment of contact or touch.

We detect the underlying facts of life: experience of the devastation of the war (the devastating Nazi war), the fate of many facing loss of mother tongue, migration, flight, the poignant attempt to find unaccented pronunciation, the fact that for many the only hope is that one might have children, as if that might fill the void of overwhelming loss.

It is as if these bodies are only barely inhabited, as if their physicality is not animated by goings on inside, as if psychical energy has ebbed, as if the performance of being human is hardly worth the effort.

Beyond this, however, lies another set of strategies, aesthetic ones.

Chantal Akerman is the child of a European cinema, the tradition of Robert Bresson: "No actors. (No directing of actors). No parts. (No learning of parts). No staging. But the use of working models, taken from life. BEING (models) instead of SEEMING (actors)." (From *Notes on Cinematography*.)

Chantal Akerman is also the child of New York, and in particular a New York where Steve Paxton and Yvonne Rainer searched for a new kind of blank performative moment. Yvonne Rainer laid down the programme: "No to spectacle No to virtuosity No to transformations and magic and make-believe No to the glamour and transcendency of the star image No to the heroic No to the antiheroic No to trash imagery No to involvement of performer or spectator No to style No to camp No to seduction of spectator by the wiles of the performer No to eccentricity No to moving or being moved."

She went on: "The challenge might be defined as how to move in the spaces between theatrical bloat with its burden of dramatic psychological 'meaning' – and – the imagery and atmospheric effects of the nondramatic, nonverbal theatre."[1]

Les Rendez-vous d'Anna can be seen as an attempt to synthesise these projects, while at the same time looking into the heart of European darkness.

Dis-moi – a break-through work by Chantal Akerman

(In support of Akerman 6, posted on *HuffPo*, 4 March 2014.)

It is doubtfuL that even the most dedicated cinephile will know *Dis-moi*, or *Aujourd'hui dis-moi*, as it is also known. It was commissioned for French TV, and has been shown only once or twice in the deepest recesses of thorough retrospectives. It has never before been subtitled for an English-speaking audience (as it will be for the screening on March 13th).

I have not found any writing at all on this film, which is hardly surprising since it is so invisible. In fact, it is invisible even by the standards of a film-maker whose great work has been woefully underrepresented even on cinémathèque screens. Nor is all her work easily available on DVD. This is odd given that she is a film-maker of the top rank, so often picked out by great film-makers for their top-ten-films-of-all-time lists.

And yet, seeing her work in chronological order in the *A Nos Amours* retrospective, as a part of an exhaustive retrospective it is immediately apparent that there is something truly exceptional happening in this slight 46-minute film made for television. It is nothing less than a reimagining of history, and the creation of a new form that Akerman has followed up on ever since.

How is this? *Dis-moi* is a set of interviews conducted by Akerman herself. We see her travel from door to door, knocking

---

[1] From: Some retrospective notes on a dance for 10 people and 12 mattresses called *Parts of Some Sextets*, performed at the Wadsworth Atheneum, Hartford, Connecticut, and Judson Memorial Church, New York, in March 1965.

and being asked in by a series of elderly, respectable-looking
ladies. She is expected. And then, over coffee and cakes, these
elderly ladies, all Jewish survivors of the Holocaust, share their
dread tales, amid diegeses about food and love and family live.
Of course the people that figure in these narratives are more
often than not dead, gassed by the Nazis.

Chantal Akerman is present in the film, as, on the one hand,
emissary of her mother, whom some of these women seem to
know well, and have known for some time, and, on the other,
as proxy for us, the viewers of the film. Chantal, a daughter, is
polite and attentive; she is a guest who clearly admires, respects,
and honours these women. What they have to say is important,
it is the stuff of life: they are sharing and rehearsing the folklore
of the tribe, they are naming their ancestors, they are showing
Chantal who she is and what she is. The terrible, ever-present
fact of the matter is the terminal disruption, the Final Solution
of the Nazis, the attempted murder of an entire race.

But this is to lapse back into a picture of the Shoah that is
not quite what this film offers. The image of the Holocaust
as an end of paternity – the eradication of sons – is potent
because it makes clear that genocide is about putting an end to
a genetic strain. It offers the image only of the end of the line.
But genocide is something else, too, it is about the disruption
of what it is that a mother gives her child, which is the living
truth, the words, the stories and a manual for life that embodies
morals, precepts and principles. Everything that defines a
culture. What we have here is a redefinition of the meaning of
genocide seen in terms of what lies behind a person, what is
inherent in lost lives lived and what has been lived through by
the survivors.

I would like to make mention of the great composer Morton
Feldman's love of Asiatic tribal rugs. He loved the uneven
regularities, the woman-made (for they all are) disruption of
mathematical certainty. One edge of a rug may figure eighteen

patterns while the other only seventeen. The thread tensions vary and the rhythms are uneven and yet beautiful. The colour repeats seem to be prone to whim, and yet taken in as a whole make perfect sense. This is how the narratives of these women come across to me in *Dis-moi*. Chantal Akerman, listening like only a psychoanalyst can listen, not compelled at all times to interrupt, to structure, to order, to make neat, permits (more, she empowers) these women to speak.

And speak they do, movingly, affectingly, wonderfully. We learn as much in these few minutes as we should about the Shoah: yes, it was a terrible crime against humanity, that needs to be remembered and memorialised, but we also learn something elemental about life in a shtetl in Poland before the war (about bakery, tailoring, courtship, love), and so therefore the truth of what is lost.

This is history as weft. The lineal facts may provide the warp, but without the weft we are unlikely to feel, because we all know what it is to sit beside a mother and hear the family history. "Eat, eat," these women urge Chantal, but they do not necessarily mean just that Chantal should eat the food. Chantal is taking communion, on what is left of the Jewish table.

There is something else to explain about this wonderful film. Chantal Akerman's mother, whose voice we hear from time to time, but never see, is herself a survivor of the Holocaust. She was sent as a child to Auschwitz along with her parents. There her parents perished, murdered by the Nazis. Chantal Akerman's mother returned, now a teenager. The ordeal is unthinkable, and this is surely a central fact of Chantal's life. To listen to one's own mother must have been, for Akerman, far from simple, mitigated only by narratives such as we listen to in *Dis-moi*: tales of shared meals, child-rearing, struggle and unexpected outcomes. These are also tales of migration and wandering, border-crossing and frontiers. And of course these are the perpetual themes in Akerman's work.

Akerman offers us something of her artist's statement: you
have to know your people's history, where you came from, in
order to know what to do next.

Chantal Akerman's *Toute une nuit* – to cleave and uncleave

(In support of Akerman 7, posted on *HuffPo*, 7 April 2014.)

Chantal Akerman's film *Toute une nuit* surprised me. I had seen
it last in a scruffy cinema in Amsterdam. It did not stick. The
images faded fast; little remained almost three decades later. It
was like a patched fresco beyond repair.

Then, in order to check the condition of a film print prior to
a run at the ICA Cinema in London, part of the *A Nos Amours*
retrospective running there until 2015 (a slow retrospective!), I sat
and discovered one of the most ravishing films I have ever seen.

What is *Toute une nuit*? It is a series of scenes, brief
encounters, chance meetings and lovers' tiffs spread across a
summer's night in Brussels. There are around 70 people, 50
scenes and not much narrative connection between them all.
What they do have in common is the wonderfully inventive,
witty, compassionate intelligence of the instigator of the scenes
– Chantal Akerman. I kept thinking of Ezra Pound's definition of
great literature: it is news that stays news. *Toute une nuit*, made
in 1982, is news, great news.

To look at the film in more detail. Here are a series of people,
some alone, some not. If they come together, they often come
together suddenly, violently, ardently. They cleave as if for the
last time. They throw arms around each other and seem unlikely
ever to let go. Or else they sit, immobile, unable to make the
first move. Glances are surreptitious, and timed to a perfection
of disconnection. If they dance (and how wonderfully they
dance!), they dance as if for the last time, clasped one to the
other, swaying in a passionate swoon. Partings can be violent,

with exits down reverberant staircases, making for a cacophony that dramatically embodies the break.

The sound world is a wonderful tapestry, woven from those sharp sounds of heels on stair and paving (no films has ever made such use of the percussive potential of women's heels!), the sound of heavy doors slammed hard, latches that resist ingress, calculating machines making a good imitation of gunfire, or even the sedative music of light rain on glass and distant thunder. When there is music, it is more than likely to be a cheesy Italian pop song blaring from a jukebox in a down-at-heel bar, where the last two drinkers are busy ignoring each other.

This nocturnal realm is a world of changes in pace and rhythm, where action is choreographed for its utility in a structure: if there has been an andante passage, then Allegro vivace is called for. If there has been complex choreographed movement in a complex interior space, then we might be offered next the contrast of a serene passage through open space. Murmured voices may repeat and iterate phrases, because the moment is inexplicably charged, as when parting or straining at cross purposes. Repetition is a formal device, but one that here carries emotional charge too.

Akerman is known for durational strategies: real-time observation of real-time processes. *Toute une nuit* does not much do that. Instead we have a set of shorter elements, arranged by proportion – a series composed of varied textures, weights and feelings. A theme and variations perhaps. Akerman and her editor find a pulse and stick to it, like good jazz. This is not about Sturm und Drang, of building up tension and releasing it, of developing anxiety then resolving it, it is about harnessing a very human love of pattern recognition, of activating a detective's instinct, of requiring of us that we take delight in a weave much like that of an Afghan rug, where the pattern is clear, yet the execution leaves room for surprise and unpredictable change. If we

could count better and hold design in mind better, we would
see better how the architect/composer had put it all together.
As it is, and film being what it is, we are in it for a while,
dependent on memory to provide perspective and overview.
We are just not very good at that. If we are lazy, we will prefer
the simplicity of an easily summarised plot outline, a clear
narrative. *Toute une nuit* is a rich feast, not suitable for the
impatient diner. It demands care and attention to fully digest.
Repeat viewings are perhaps desirable.

I wonder about precedents for what seems to me a wholly
original work. I think of Max Ophüls' *La Ronde*, where perhaps
the most interesting connection with *Toute une nuit* is not that
both films offer a series of scenes with no one protagonist, but
the fact that Ophüls and Akerman both are concerned with the
physical presence of actors, constrained by physical tasks and
time, rather than what the camera and editing can do. I am
reminded, too, of Astaire and Rogers strolling in Central Park,
only to fall into step and dance in *The Band Wagon*.

And finally, what of cleaving and uncleaving? These are
wonderfully ambiguous terms. To cleave means to both
part and at the same time to join. Watching Akerman's
protagonists cleaving unto one another, is to see that they are
only too aware that only time will tell, that nothing is forever,
that the moment is always tinged with tragedy because it will
pass. Just as a pair of lovers seem absolutely joined and lost
in a poetic flight of utter, blissful union, a phone rings, day
breaks and the soundtrack fades. Traffic noise intrudes loudly.
Morning has broken. Cleaving makes way for uncleaving. And
vice versa.

Chantal Akerman's *Les Années 80* – a film about spinning

(In support of Akerman 8, posted on *HuffPo*, 24 April 2014.)

Halfway through a retrospective of Chantal Akerman's films.
Surely surprise and innovation are exhausted. Seeing *Les Années
80* proves otherwise. This film is rare: it is not available on DVD,
and the only print with English subtitles is on its last legs.

It begins with voices heard over black – the voice of an actor
and a director, trying to find the right intonation for a short
enigmatic phrase: "A ton âge, un chagrin, c'est vite passé" –
meaning, "At your age sorrows soon pass", or maybe, "At your
age misery doesn't last". The inflection required, perhaps
because meaning must be found, proves elusive. Later in the
film, when we hear the phrase used, it sneaks up on us, deep
in context. But here, listening to voices, disembodied, as if
heard in a Beckett radio play, we get into the to and fro between
the women, the work being done, the sense of a search, of a
collaboration. Women are speaking, but we don't see them. The
things that happen when we see women onscreen – fall into the
charged world of the image – can't happen. Instead we listen.

The first thing we do see are women's ankles, in a range of
footwear, walking, flitting past, parading, striding, prancing. The
rhythms are choreographed and edited beautifully. We are looking at
women, having already been set up to know that this is a film about
how women can relate, work together, and do so within the confines
of particular and specific forms of cultural expression. The women
we see are finding performances. They are looking for a self that fits.
The director, by the same token, is also finding her role.

These feet and their movement are the start of a careful
assembly of video footage, labelled as "auditions". Dialogue
is trialled, songs recorded, guide tracks laid down, costumes
tested, and movement invented. The voice of the director is
often present. The director is sometimes in frame, conducting,
urging, encouraging, questioning.

There is some structuring of this material into broad
categories: this is no mere exercise in taxonomy (no mere
shuffling of material into kinds), it is a delightful play, a
sublimely edited and judged chequerboard of durations,
weights and proportions. This "auditions" section reveals the act
of making, of spinning (to use the terms as conceived by Mary
Daly), of women (in the main) working together to inhabit the
dialogue that teeters on the brink of kitsch, working with the
elements of melodrama, of situations that could become clichéd,
but which never become so because of the rapport that we
witness - rapport between those who know they are there to be
looked at, and must inhabit the roles expected of them, become
the objects of our visual desire. We must want to look, and they
must want us to look.

To round things off, we are treated to a sequence shot on
35mm film, now sharp and better lit. This is a set of try-out song
and dance numbers. A melodramatic narrative, something about
one woman's love of a man but who loves another, threads
things together, and lends the expected musical dramatic sense
to the numbers.

The performers are not always the ones we expected – the
auditions have not prepared us for the final casting, even if there
is such a thing. The concept that the actor and the role are one
is never allowed to take root. That is one avant-garde strategy
that undercuts genre convention. Though these film sequences
look dressed and staged, they nevertheless have the feel of
screen tests, something not finished, depending on jump cuts to
put things together, disrupting classical cinema norms. But the
sheer visual pleasure of better lit film after an hour of video is
something to relish.

The close of the film offers a break from the confines of
rehearsal room and the locations of the 35mm song and
dance sequences: the camera is now on a roof high above
Brussels at dusk. It pans all the way round several times, while

Akerman's voice recites the list of those she wants to thank, and
promises, "Next year in Jerusalem" – the close of the Jewish
Seder, conveying a sense of closure, but also of yearning and
of impossible dreaming. We return to darkness for a music play
out – the orchestrated tune we are by now very familiar with,
a jaunty tune that feels just right for the 80s: brash, bright,
superficial. It is the kind of tune that sticks, and which will
annoy some.

There is a very prosaic reason for the making of this film – *Les
Années 80*. Akerman wanted to raise money for a film musical,
which was slated to be titled *Toison d'Or* (the name of the
vast shopping mall where she intended to shoot – meaning
The Golden Fleece) and needed to raise a significant budget.
Her previous work, being essentially experimental, albeit
supported by celebrity actors (Delphine Seyrig had championed
and helped secure finance the *Jeanne Dielman* project) was
presumably a poor calling card. To shoot a full-blown musical
with a large cast on location would be something else. *Les
Années 80* did the trick. Two years later *Golden Eighties*, with
Delphine Seyrig, Fanny Cottençon, Aurore Clément and others
was shot.

But this is a film to look at on its own terms. To return to
spinning. Spinning is about the drawing out and twisting
together of threads to make a yarn. The threads twisting against
each other produce the thread that does not unravel, and has
strength far greater than the threads themselves. Spinning is
women's work – and as Mary Daly suggested, spinning is what
radical feminists can do to produce meanings and identities
beyond those allowed by patriarchy: women are instructed to
jettison old forms, to resist the demand for closure, make new
forms, and cut through "the mazes of man-made mystification,
breaking the mind-bindings of master-minded double think"
(such is the delightful phrasing of Daly's *Gyn/Ecology!*).

And, so it seems to me, this is just what *Les Années 80* is all about: occupying the bastion of melodramatic expression and emotionalism, revealing and revelling in its synthetic and artificial nature, highlighting the silly ease of looking at screened women playing roles, and then playing and making merry in a newly revealed universe. And what a surprising, challenging and yet refreshing pleasure it is to look and share in such richness.

Chantal Akerman: questions about duration

(In support of Akerman 9 and 10, posted on *ICA Bulletin*, 20 May 2014.)

The next two instalments of the Chantal Akerman retrospective will consist of shorter works: *Programme 9* includes two one-hour films, while *Programme 10* includes five short films. This is not a grouping for convenience, but is a reflection of what Akerman worked on in the 1980s – mainly short work made for television in France.

A question immediately presents itself: why would a celebrated film-maker decide to work on a miniature scale after delivering a series of long-form works, including the magisterial *Jeanne Dielman* which runs at 201 minutes?

Why, then, the assumption that a film-maker should start short and go long? In the field of poetry, long lyrical poems are not now so admired: rather the concision of the sonnet, or several stanzas of a page or two are much preferred. Who reads *Childe Harold* when *She Walks in Beauty* is so good and so short?

Tastes change, but the standardisation of the feature film length appears unassailable (even if 90 minutes has now been supplanted by 110 or even 120 minutes). Rare to find a film of 80-odd minutes, enough to merit comment in any review. It is of course only in the commercial cinema that 'feature length' is the standard unit of measure. Film as an art practice and as a medium for gallery exhibition has never felt such constraint. Both Michael Snow and Andy Warhol (whose work Akerman

came to know very early on in her life as a film-maker) produced
works of wildly varied length: Snow with *Wavelength* at 45
minutes and *La Région centrale* at 180 minutes, Warhol with
any *Screen Test* at 2½ minutes and *Empire* at 485 minutes.

Why did Akerman go short? A few real world issues were
surely impinging on her artistic ambitions.

The 1980s were far from easy times. Indeed, Akerman's film *Les
Années 80* and later *Golden Eighties* were overt about this: times
were tough. Recession and oil shocks dominated the economics
of the decade. Film producers were obliged to cut their cloth.
Akerman was focused on financing *Golden Eighties*, a project
with a large cast, with ambitious production values, and likely
to be in need of widespread release to recoup costs. Akerman
has often doubled as producer on her projects, and this must
have consumed time and energy. The film was released in 1986,
and despite some compromises on the budget, was every bit as
high-profile and lavish as intended. The short films shot around
this time, those included in *Akerman 9* and *10*, might well be a
measure of the time available to Akerman, of the need to take
advantage of small-scale, readily achieved commissions.

It is also worth noting that the 80s were fertile times for
short-form TV commissioning, generally shot on 16mm and
shown together in curatorial strands or portfolio formats.
This happened in France, as in the UK when Channel 4
came into being. For example, *Un Jour Pina a demandé* was
commissioned as part of a series called '*Repères sur la modern
dance*'; *Lettre de cinéaste* was part of series called '*Cinéma
cinémas*'; and *Family Business* was commissioned as part of the
Visions strand on Channel 4.

These shorter works present distinct possibilities. They are
not required to deliver a comprehensive view. They can be, and
often are, formally inventive, gnomic, quizzical, incomplete,
mysterious, enigmatic… They take risks with audiences that
simply would not be taken working in long-form.

A good example is the short film *Le marteau* (*The Hamme*r,
seen in *Akerman 10*). This is a four-minute film from 1986,
shot for French Television, ostensibly about the artist Jean-Luc
Vilmouth. The hammer is the tool a sculptor uses to chip away
at the block; it is, for Vilmouth, emblematic and he has made the
outline of a mason's hammer his icon. Akerman here instigates
a game of musical chairs, as if the loss of a chair and the removal
of participants reflect the artist chipping away at a block. The
winner, the person emblematic perhaps of a sculptural form,
is then permitted to take a hammer from a wall (where it has
been displayed as kind of artwork in relief) and hurl it out into
the starry night. The hammer whirls and twirls against the stars,
the strings that hold it aloft quite visible. In other words, an
intensely elliptical, oddly fascinating work.

These shorter works of Akerman's contain marvels. *L'Homme
à la valise* is very funny, a beautifully composed study in
psychological warfare that Buster Keaton would have approved
of. *Lettre de cinéaste* is a playful antidote to any expectation of
highbrow seriousness from the author of *Jeanne Dielman*. *J'ai
faim, j'ai froid* is a physical comedy offering zestful rhythmical
play, and may just be an autobiographical fragment. *Un Jour
Pina a demandé* is a wonderful encounter between two women
artists, a work that has been far too infrequently seen.

Short forms and miniatures can be symbolic in a way that
long form may not be. There is something about a microcosm
that can bear the weight of ponderous significance better than
a longer work, where nuance and delicacy are prized. In a
short film there is no expectation that meaning will be made
clear by the end of the work. Short allows digestion at leisure:
short forms can be inexplicable, a time bomb of meaning set to
detonate later on. Short can be a tatty affair that need not dress
itself up in fine clothes. We allow short forms to be provisional,
not quite sure of themselves. We allow short form to short
change us.

Unfettered expression: Chantal Akerman's *Golden Eighties*

(In support of *Akerman 11, ICA Bulletin*, 17 July 2014)

Chantal Akerman and Delphine Seyrig had worked together
once before – in the magisterial, astonishing *Jeanne Dielman,
23 Quai du Commerce, 1080 Bruxelles* (1975). Now, in *Golden
Eighties* they work together again, this time to make a musical
shot in the bubble-gum tones of Fujicolor, bursting with pithy,
catchy songs and melodramatic scenes of heartbreak and
anguished longing for a better life. Restraint has been replaced
by unfettered expression – or so it seems. Seyrig's character
(again called 'Jeanne') is married, working in the Toison d'Or
shopping mall, a long-suffering wife trapped behind a counter.
Perhaps she is Jeanne Dielman some years later. Let's hope her
husband has hidden the scissors.

Why would a film-maker make such a journey from austere
art-house to exuberant genre film? The answer perhaps lies
in the life represented in the Toison d'Or – everything is for
sale, everything is desirable if beautifully presented in a shop
window, if desire is about how one looks, how one presents
oneself. This is after all the 80s – golden or not depending on
your outlook.

The film also makes very clear that the 1980s are a time
of economic difficulty – where businesses are failing, where
customers are scarce, where only the fittest will survive – and
there is no alternative world view on offer. Everything is for sale,
if only someone would buy.

And yet, *Golden Eighties* is no hymn of praise to consumerism
and neoconservative ideology. It is a film that offers no ready
identifications or point of view. To watch this film is to be busy
working out the relationships, the backstories, the internal
structures of trust and affection. Yes the film presents a range
of (mainly) women fixated on romance and love, yet the
dramatic closures on offer lie not in pairing off with the man of

a woman's dreams (disappointment seems all that follows from that!) but in the comfort of women friends, women colleagues, singing and dancing together. Men are either absent, faithless, or callow, insincere. Better that men stay in women's dreams. Women, on the other hand…

This is of course an oversimplification. But the pressing question remains: what kind of pleasure is Akerman proposing in *Golden Eighties*? The surface is very much in contrast to the austere regimes of *Jeanne Dielman*, where once there were subdued colours, long, durational shots, an absence of close-ups, formal framings, use of off-screen sound, and careful structuring of time and sequence, now there is a busy, colourful world, with emotions expressed, hearts worn on sleeves. *Golden Eighties* is also a delightful confection of ironic play, a delightful teasing of cliché. Akerman is like an expert chef, tossing pancakes at the tableside, presenting a perfectly folded crêpe

What, though, of the vampish Lili? She is the object of desire in the mall: the boys sing of her, she breaks hearts, choses who she will seduce. She provokes the onscreen chorus to sing like a Greek chorus, commenting on her duplicity, her allure, her command. That is a strategy that develops a complicity between viewer and authorial intelligence. Moreover, this film may also be one of the first releases intended for mainstream distribution where certain protagonists repeatedly catch the camera's eye: a strategy that unsettles like no other.

Akerman, raising a significant budget for *Golden Eighties* (her first truly commercial project), moved into the shopping mall but made it her own – a realm of avant-garde activity: authored, mediated, disenchanted, wise – but also fun, wicked and compassionate. She has a sense of the potential pleasures and satisfactions of cinema but the wit to maintain her intellectual grip.

Laugh or cry: Jewish humour in Chantal Akerman's *Histoires d'Amérique*

(In support of Akerman 13, posted on *ICA Bulletin*, 22 October 2014.)

Chantal Akerman's film of 1989 *Histoires d'Amérique*, which Akerman herself subtitled in English as 'Food, Family and Philosophy', was not highly rated by Jonathan Rosenbaum: "Akerman is basically geared toward interiors, which may be one reason her latest feature, Food, Family and Philosophy, set mostly in exteriors, is not one of her strongest".

It is true that Akerman is brilliant when confronted by narrow doorways, small rooms, and constricted passageways. Her 1983 short film *L'Homme à la valise* is a miracle of improvisation in an impossibly tight location. But to suppose that physical constraint is all that holds humans in bondage is surely a mistake. The weight of history, of a sense of dread, anxiety, or that annihilation is just around the corner are as real as walls, not least if you have fled pogrom and Holocaust, or left behind those who were not so lucky as you.

To survive can be terrible.

Akerman begins *Histoires* with a shot of Manhattan across the water. Mist and fading light. The upper storeys of the city's skyscrapers are lost in the murk. The camera seems to stalk the city - an inversion of the view we had at the end of *News from home*, the last film Akerman shot in New York, where the ferry from which she filmed was heading away from Manhattan. She provides the voiceover:

"A rabbi always passed through a village to get to the forest, and there, at the foot of a tree (and it was always the same one) he began to pray and God heard him. His son, too, always passed through the village but he could not remember where the tree was, and so he prayed at the foot of any old tree and God heard him. His grandson did not know where the tree was, nor the forest, but went to pray in the village and God heard him. His great-grandson did not know where the tree was, nor the forest, not even the village, but he still knew the words of the prayer, and so he prayed in his house and God heard him. His great-great-grandson did not know where the tree, nor the forest, nor the village were, not even the words of the prayer, but he still knew the story and told it to his children; and God heard him."

That sets up what follows. The jokes, stories, skits and silences are the verbal survivals of European Jewish culture, cast up by diaspora on these shores, preserving certain forms of life in the shtetls and cities of the lost old world.

What to expect? – mordant wisdom, resignation, perky resistance and opportunism. The cast of the film are found on the streets and corners of their adopted, run-down city (as it was then), eventually on an abandoned plot in Brooklyn, with the city lights of Manhattan in the distance. Shades of *Waiting for Godot*, shades of Isaac Bashevis Singer's shtetl tales, shades of the badchen of the Old Country (the jesters hired to add vim to Ashkenazi weddings before Nazis put an end to that world).

Akerman recruited a varied cast, some professional comedians, some not. Some were old, some not. All are Jewish of the first and second generations. All have jokes, stories and anecdotal proof that something has persisted, something that defines has survived, despite loss and trauma and death.

Above all, Akerman's acutely musical sense of time, rhythm and change is present. Her sense of when to cut, when not to cut, when to close in, when to hold back, defines her method. She is the most musical of film-makers.

Shot on film, 16mm intended to be printed onto 35mm stock, the negatives and all prints, Akerman tells us, are now lost. This Beta SP copy is the surviving copy – a jaded videotape with French subtitles burned in (the soundtrack is in English, with Yiddish vocabulary thrown in ad lib). The survival of this film has become something in need of a prayer.

Chantal Akerman: film-making as composing

(in support of Akerman 14, posted on *HuffPo*, 11 November 2014.)

Looking forward to a screening of three rarely seen films by Chantal Akerman. What might a film-maker learn from music?

Music is a source of primal pleasures, pleasures such as rhythm (things happening regularly), counterpoint (things happening simultaneously), tune and melody. Music cuts across all cultures, nationalities, it cancels gender and so wonderfully infects every living human soul.

Film has its own unique properties but looking at three superb shorter films by Chantal Akerman, side-by-side (as by chance they will be in our ongoing, chronological retrospective in London) makes very clear that for Akerman – perhaps more than for any other film-maker – film-making is an act of composition. I would argue that this is the key to understanding Akerman's remarkable and completely commanding style.

Film, to generalise, chases the story, chases the white rabbit of action. To frame is to frame an action; to cut is to pursue a change; to move from wide shot to close up is to close in on what is of interest. Akerman is not like that. Akerman, to make use of Tarkovsky's useful notion, sculpts time. She works with rhythm, pulse and counterpoint. She choreographs bodily movement as if working with dancers, creating patterns that have more to do with timing than narrative. I would like to say she composes, makes tunes and lays them out in time. I imagine a musical score capturing the essence of her films than would a dialogue transcript.

Akerman has a keen ear for music, and music figures directly in many of her films. In *Les Années 80* she entered the frame to conduct her singer. She even sings a song herself. It is also clear, from her earliest work that Akerman is acutely aware of the value of sound. The percussive footsteps of *Jeanne Dielman* do not fade from memory long after viewing. Indeed in many ways

sound defines that film. Silence as a value is something that
her musically inflected sensibility well understands. If Akerman
decides to play a film or passage mute, it is for a good reason.

Sonia Wieder-Atherton is a cellist of the top rank, and since
the early 80s, a key collaborator. First seen in an enigmatic
short entitled *Rue Mallet-Stevens*, Wieder-Atherton is both
protagonist and performer. In the first of the three short films
in the programme, a film called *Trois strophes sur le nom
de Sacher*, Wieder-Atherton enters, cello in hand, and sits to
perform the music by Henri Dutilleux. These are the three
strophes (sometimes called stanzas) that give the film its name.
The music was written originally for Mstislav Rostropovich,
who had asked a number of composers to offer something
to celebrate the birthday of Paul Sacher, a much-loved Swiss
conductor. This is extraordinary music: a sonatina of beguiling,
sinuous and utterly disarming simplicity. Wieder-Atherton,
naturally, performs this with complete focus and poise, her
cello tuned to other worldly scales.

But Akerman is a film-maker, and this is no mere
documentary, though superficially it may seem so. Akerman
places Wieder-Atherton in a room, with drapes, evoking a
proscenium arch. In the background are windows, looking
across to the wall and windows of another building. The
windows reveal other rooms, interiors, with inhabitants.
These characters appear and disappear, coming and going.
They interact, in plays of minimalist gestures, meticulous
choreographies. The music, the performance, the actions are a
carefully organised counterpoint (counterpoint, by the way, is
usually defined as the relationship between parts or voices that
are interdependent harmonically yet independent in rhythm and
contour). And that is exactly what Akerman works with. There
is no narrative intent, though narrative may be guessed at: no
chasing of actions and incident, no hierarchy of interest. It is a
film built around a structure, a very musical structure.

The second film of the three is essentially performance/ lecture – a masterclass by one of the greatest pianists of any age, Alfred Brendel. Brendel talks us through the harmonic world of the three last piano sonatas by Schubert. He talks of the music's melodic charms and relationship with the work of other masters. He touches on the fact these are Schubert's three last works for piano, but points out that Schubert could not have known when he wrote them that they would be last works. He also relates how these works were not performed in Schubert's day, how they were then lost, only later to be recovered, and, in modern times, their nature and importance as compositions grasped and now are taken for granted.

Brendel's manner throughout is calm, as he talks with a lofty authority that permits him a striking simplicity and directness. Akerman's film-making is in the same vein – simple, direct, nuanced, rhythmical without excessive force or emphasis. Every edit is perfectly judged, the ebb and flow of attention perfectly supportive. This is a film in tune. It is a musically felicitous construction – that allows the insights of Brendel's talk to shine through. Akerman's restraint is that of an accompanist who knows she must support the soloist, and yet success always depends on balance.

Incidentally, Brendel talks about Schubert making his music in relative obscurity, depending on knowledgeable salon audiences for commissions and appreciation. Schubert lived and worked in the shadow of the hugely successful Ludwig van Beethoven. Schubert famously called for a Beethoven string quartet to be performed at his bedside as he lay dying. Is this for Akerman analogous to how she might regard Jean-Luc Godard, whom she references constantly and in whose shadow all film-makers must exist?

The third film in this set of films is *Le Déménagement*, shot for Arte, the French TV station, one of a series of monologues from various film-makers. Akerman wrote the script for this film herself. She makes use of a restrained number of angles of a man in his new home, but who has yet to unpack because he is afflicted by uncertainty and doubt.

"I should never, never have moved. What got into me? I was happy before. Well, almost. No, mostly I was not. Not good at all. I had to move".

This is a densely woven soliloquy of indecision, of regret, of a sense of predicament that is inescapable. Through this protagonist, Akerman reflects on the impossibility of making decisions, of the forlorn hope of certainty. It is a project that seems to owe much to Samuel Beckett, that great dramatist of endless indecision.

But what strikes the viewer is the patterning of the shots, the frequent cuts to black, of the rhythm and pacing of the text. Sami Frey's performance of this man imprisoned by existential despair is remarkable, a bravura performance, depending on subtle control of voice and timbre. His control is absolute as he works within Akerman's structure. He provides the audible pulse, while Akerman works with image and timing. The past is a prison that must be remembered and raked over forever, for there is nothing else.

This is to say that the music Akerman conjures up is an inescapable melody, composed with such precision, that to start is to be held (surely?) in its grip until the close.

In the Schubert film Brendel says that he finds in the sonatas by Schubert "a combination of the formal and psychological as there should be in all great music". That is exactly what I would say is to be found in all of Akerman's work: a happy combination of the formal and psychological.

These three accidentally juxtaposed films, of varying unconventional durations, prove to be a perfect, illuminating demonstration of Akerman's art.

Travelling shots in Chantal Akerman's *D'Est*
(*From the East*, 1993)

(In support of Akerman 16, posted on *HuffPo*, 21 January 2015.)

I asked Chantal what kind of conversations she would typically have with dolly grips about tracking shots in her movies. What do you mean? she said. We use a car and shoot out of the window! I was astonished, but then Chantal resists the usual kind of conversations about film.

First of all, what is a 'dolly grip', in case you don't know what that is? A 'dolly' is the platform on wheels or whatever that runs along rails and allows the smooth movement of a heavy camera for film-making. The most famous dolly is the one supposedly invented by Fred Astaire and his team to follow his dance – in fact a huge dolly with complex crane contraption that allowed the camera to shoot low, or high, move forward and back as well as side to side, so that whatever he did the camera could follow. The names of the dolly team on *Top Hat* are not credited onscreen (you would need to see the call sheets stored somewhere in the RKO vaults to find that out), and yet the films are memorable because of the faultless work of the dolly grips, who judged the speed of the 'move to follow' (the phrase camera teams generally use), the coming to rest, the start of a move and the rhythm of it all to a tee. Oddly, seamless and choreographic movement of the camera such as this is becomes invisible because it is rooted in choreographed bodily movements.

What the camera sees and how it can move-to-follow was perhaps a familiar experience before even the advent of cinema: that is to anyone who has tried to conjure and hold an image in the mind – just close your eyes and imagine your walk to work. If a camera move is done well, we don't notice what a miracle it is. It is far from easy to move a camera around smoothly and in graceful fashion. (At the time *Top Hat* was shot, a camera could weighed in at several hundredweight.) It is just as far from easy to imagine walking around a vividly conceived cloister in a memory exercise, with reliably placed niches and corners which serve to trigger recall. The link between kinds of movement in these two realms seems to connect for me.

Moreover, that a movie camera moves for me evokes something of how the mind works – to hold something in the mind's eye is often to have to imagine a varying perspective on that thing. Still won't do.

Early cinema was intrigued by the 'phantom ride', the view from the front of a train or vehicle moving forward through the world. Such a subjective experience would have been most beguiling: an instantly comprehended filmic representation evoking a familiar first-person movement through an environment. Indeed, speedy movement of a subjective point of view and a privileged world view are still the main sell that cinema has to offer.

But beyond such primitive, mesmeric allure, what about the movement of the camera? What if movement is not motivated by the demand to follow a human body in movement or to suggest a privileged spectatorship?

Chantal Akerman's work is far removed from that of Fred Astaire, of course. She is a single person, an auteur, a film-maker in complete charge of the process, deciding where the camera goes, what it sees, and what happens in front of it. Sometimes she chooses even to appear in her own films. Mostly, her camera stays put, offering unblinking framing of spaces and entrances to spaces. Corridors and doorways are her frequent material. Akerman has, to generalise, been concerned with structuring what her stationary camera records. Perhaps budget constraints and artistic purposes happily coincided.

What of camera movement in Akerman's work? *Hotel Monterey* includes the suggestion of camera movement when shooting inside a lift reveals movement in the slit window of the lift as it ascends. Later, her camera creeps forward, then retreats in one of the narrow hotel corridors – a kind of 'phantom ride'. She panned the camera in one 360° shot then back in the reverse direction in *La Chambre*. The camera reframes and holds choreographed movement in *Les Années 80* and *Golden Eighties*. The camera dollies in slightly in *Le Déménagement*. While the camera is permitted its own motivation, not until her film *D'Est* of 1993 would the camera become a protagonist, in the way that had become familiar as a trope of art-house cinema in the later 60s and onwards. But as ever, Akerman is like no other film-maker, and *D'Est* moves seamlessly across genres, across modes of representation and without a bump into a new kind of cinema – one in which camera movement is central.

D'Est is outwardly a 16mm documentary shot in Poland, East Germany (GDR) and the USSR, shot on trips taken as the Soviet system was about to collapse. Akerman has said she went 'while there was still time'. What kind of time, or whose time, or if there is any elsewhere (the suggestion may be that there is not!), I do not know. The film, however, avoids dialogue of any kind – though people often enough exchange words, they are not audible, and never subtitled. This is not silent film, however, as the world is a noisy one, and one where cheesy pop music and stirring tunes play from speakers and loudspeakers. Dancing is allowed. The people in this film are seen to exist. We don't know their stories.

Akerman alternates between existence in public spaces and in private spaces. She alternates day and night. And she alternates static shots with moving shots – but not just any old travelling shots.

Akerman moves her camera along rows of people, along paths and lines. Her purpose is not narrative. If, for example, people are lined up waiting for a bus, then to travel along the line is not about narrative, though time and space are conflated – to wait is to be in a physical relationship with a row of others. To travel along that row of bodies is to discover the time invested. In other words, it is a narrative about waiting, a narrative we know that is about waiting for regime change, about ends of worlds, about existential uncertainty.

I suspect these sequences are haunted by the European memory of lines of people, not knowing where they are going, at the mercy of system that may have a final solution in mind. Railways can never be neutral in the European imagination, especially the imagination of a person whose mother was an Auschwitz survivor.

What is extraordinary about Akerman's travelling shots is that they do not lead to a reveal (the term is used by film folk to talk about a moment of discovery for the audience). Hollywood, with its concern with obstacles and the overcoming of obstacles, seems to me to structure all movement as a search and a revealing discovery, while Akerman never builds to climax, or payoff. The movements are very even, without accent, and do not have the feeling of a movement towards or away from anything. To predict when they will end is a fool's errand.

Akerman has said she shoots from moving cars – and that may be why the view perpendicular to the direction of travel is the invariable condition of her travelling shots in *D'Est*. But associations spring to mind for such shooting.

I think of tableau vivant, which describes a group of costumed actors or models, posed and often theatrically lit. These figures do not speak or move. The set-up is a collision of the stage and painting or photography. In this way, *D'Est* can be seen as a reversion to the primitive and essential condition of cinema before film was invented.

I am also reminded of religious paintings and frescos in which the image must be read from left to right or right to left to produce a chronology of, say, a saintly life. Events are simultaneously represented and yet they are intended to be

experienced sequentially, not as a series of discrete images
and moments, but as an emotional journey through a familiar
set of incarnations. The bodily movement required of the
spectator is critical (a crabwise shimmy) – which, to me, is
evoked when watching the moving shots in *D'Est* – a sense
of traversing.

A traverse – not the most familiar camera movement in film
history. To traverse means to go sideways, not to confront, or
take control of, not to penetrate, not to withdraw. To traverse is
to allow, to accept, to tolerate. To traverse is to move around the
body of something that must be respected, that is not exactly a
barrier but is not invaded. I like this move because it is— to veer
into the metaphorical – feminine. It is as if clinging to something
vast and unknowable, not to an object but to a feeling. There is
always more…

No one who appears in the shot is privileged, no one in
particular is picked out – all are equal, all are deserving, all are
as real as any other. All are deserving of pity as any other. To put
it another way – the movement, the film-making is democratic.
When a cut to another shot comes, there is no correct moment
to do that, though it always feels right in hindsight that a change
has come. For *D'Est*, Akerman was working with editors Claire
Atherton and Agnès Bruckert. Every decision is the right one,
and that in itself deserves attention.

It is a miracle of Akerman's films generally that she has never
made an error of judgment about duration of shots or scenes.
She may test patience and endurance but hindsight always
vindicates the decisions. Other film-makers may work with long,
sustained shots, but as I see it, they are led by action that they
have carefully designed, and carefully follow. Their purpose
is narrative or expositional. They do not have such a subtle
interest in the status of the film image itself and the structuring
of experience. Nor does it seem relevant to me that others
have made work in which every single shot is of great duration

and which offers almost no overt narrative material (a recent
favourite of mine is *Unser täglich Brot* by Nikolaus Geyrhalter),
for this is not to work structurally but to embrace a certain
aesthetic manner – which is a matter of tone not tune.

To go back to Astaire: he danced and his dance structured
the world of *Top Hat*; Akerman structures the world and that is
her dance.

On Chantal Akerman

(In support of Akerman 25, posted *ICA Bulletin*, 19 October 2015.)

Chantal Akerman loved Joseph Conrad, and that's not
surprising. He was the writer that looked most unsparingly into
the colonial heart of darkness. Chantal Akerman was perhaps,
of all film-makers born just after the war, the most sensible to
the horror of it all: some may have analysed or looked more
directly at the legacy and experiences of war and Holocaust, but
Akerman registered the reverberations, the traumatic aftermath,
the backwash like no other. Akerman well understood how the
contemporary world has been shaped by the pervasive after-
effects of the horror.

Conrad's *Almayer's Folly*, set in Borneo, tells the story of a
planter whose dreams of easy riches fail, leaving him to take
comfort in opium amid the ruin of his splendid but absurd
upriver home – his Folly. Akerman is not about to let her
colonial opportunist off so easily, for opium is to numb the pain,
and Akerman, daughter of a Holocaust survivor, did not believe
in sedation.

The tragic news of Akerman's death leaves us to contemplate
Almayer's Folly in a new, sombre light. When she was alive,
there might yet have been another cinema work of fiction.
Indeed, she was writing a script for one. While she was alive,
the film stood as another marker along the way, there was the

expectation of another. Now, suddenly, it is a terminal work.
There is a documentary still to come (*No Home Movie*, 2015),
but in terms of a scripted, conceived and executed cinema film
on 35mm film stock, this is it.

We may perhaps want now to think of the film as in some way
characteristic 'late Akerman' – a notion of Adorno's widely taken
up but questioned by Akerman in her film about Schubert's
last sonatas. As Alfred Brendel (the great pianist who plays and
speaks so brilliantly in the film) points out, Schubert did not
know when he composed the sonatas that they would be last
works. The film asked us to think hard about the pitfalls of such
sentimental retrospection.

And now we must look in retrospect at *La Folie Almayer*.
Might we incline to seeing the film as a comment on the
condition of cinema – cinema perhaps as failed colonialist
adventure in search of fool's gold?

Akerman liked to shoot on film, but had lately given that up
– she is credited as one of the producers of *La Folie Almayer*
and complained to me about the sheer horror of raising
money for such expensive film-making (in this case financed
by means of a complex of tax breaks and multinational co-
production). Indeed, her last work was shot on video, some
of it even on her BlackBerry phone (the brilliantly expressive
and resonant first shot of *No Home Movie*, in particular). She
loved working without needing a crew, being able to travel and
shoot at will, without a budget spreadsheet. Indeed, when she
worked alone, she could produce a work like *Là-bas*, a daring,
brilliantly conceived film that seems now like one of her
absolute high points.

To wallow in sentimental retrospect, or to coolly assess the
body of work taken as a whole in necessary academic study, or
to prophylactically stitch such dangerous and radical work as
hers safely into dusty obituary, ready to be filed in inaccessible
archives, or make use of her for purposes yet to be revealed is

all very well and inevitable, but I am left just now simply with the horrible fact of Chantal's absence. She was a towering spirit, an intelligence that cinema desperately needed – no, make that needs now more than ever.

It is finally important to underline how interesting a two-year, slow retrospective has been. It has been for all of us who have been able to attend and think about the work quite the most remarkable privilege. The films we looked at were made over a 40-year span. We took in them in at rate that seemed right. At the start we feared a loss of appetite or falling away of interest – but the reverse has been true. To see not so well known films, and to see them away from the proximity and fanfare of the better-known work, revealed that conventional assessments are often faulty or inadequate. To see films in the company of others is to see them better and more clearly. To see films in the order that they were made has been often a delightful surprise.

The 'slow retrospective' is surely now a proven concept?

RIP Chantal Akerman
6 June 1950 – 5 October 2015

Press articles

BY JOANNA HOGG AND ADAM ROBERTS

Chantal Akerman: extraordinary artist of the everyday who we will miss forever

The Guardian, Thursday 8 October 2015.

With heavy hearts we have tried to gather our thoughts. Our perspective is hard to describe; in curating Chantal's work, we came to know her personally. And in doing so we discovered that Chantal's films and Chantal herself are, in so many ways, the same thing. She eschewed categorisation – as an artist, as a female film-maker. She was simply Chantal Akerman.

Some people will be wondering who Chantal Akerman was. She ought not need an introduction – she is a film-maker who changed what cinema is or could be or ought to be. She strode effortlessly into the roll-call of great auteurs, her work into the lists of best films ever made.

And yet her films are hard to see. Hence our idea to stage a complete retrospective in London; two years of screenings allowing us and many regulars to fall in love with her work. When Chantal visited us, unannounced, last year, she was greeted by this community with joy and open arms. We treasure a memory of the spontaneous standing ovation in a packed ICA. She was surprised and delighted. Had she never before received such a warm welcome?

Month by month through these screenings, we witnessed her life, her ideas, her innermost thoughts. Now, she's so under our skin that our own experiences have become entwined with hers. A tearful moment, thinking of one's own parent, is well-hidden in the darkness of the cinema while Chantal reads on-screen letters written by her mother in *News from home* (1976). A difficult, grey London day ends with song and dance in her featherlight musical *Golden Eighties* (1983), its catchy signature tune in our heads for days afterwards.

Even if sometimes we have felt frustrated because such immersion in someone else's work has had an impact on our own, we have been enriched and inspired by the never-ending outpouring of creativity. Every film is treasure, rich in personal detail, autobiographical fact, intelligent and playful reconfiguration of genre and expectation. They are poised critiques of knowledge and power, a series of love letters to cinema, a flow of movement, choreography and drama unparalleled in the work of any other individual film artist.

Her love of music provides one way to think of her delicious and dextrous weaving of the threads of every component of a film; as a composer weaves melodies, pitches and rhythms, so she weaves movement, time, duration, edits, sounds and silences. No work is negligible: some are symphonic, suitable for large-scale exhibition, while some are solo sonatas, or even miniature chamber pieces. As with Bach, one should never dismiss a work of even a few bars.

She never rested. She travelled widely, thought about injustice, went where the poorest lived, interviewed them, made feature films, documentaries, short-form dramas, gnomic shorts, musicals, and artworks that could amplify in new ways her preoccupation with ephemerality, liminality, loss, disappearance, memory and sanctity.

Her work finds loveliness in everyday life, everyday objects, everyday tasks, but sees also the horror that can be overlooked under the veneer of the commonplace. When she made a musical, she set it in a mall where shopkeepers struggle with the economic realities of failing businesses. When she made a comedy about an unwanted house guest, it is the ordinary sounds and habits of that guest in another room that intrude so

comically on the writing of a film script. When a house must be
sold in a broad Lubitsch-like comedy, one prospective buyer of
the house sympathises with the vendor as "second generation" -
that is, the children of Holocaust survivors.

Her masterpiece, *Jeanne Dielman, 23 Quai du Commerce,
1080 Bruxelles* – made when she was 25, younger than
Orson Welles was when he made *Citizen Kane* – is apparently
about a middle-aged widow, who goes about a meticulously
ordered domestic life, making ends meet through carefully
compartmentalised acts of prostitution. It is also the fruit of
a loving, sympathetic yet penetrating observation of her own
mother's humdrum habits as she defended herself against
the horrors she had known (Nelly Akerman was deported to
Auschwitz as a child, where her parents and many of her family
were murdered). Love does not imply blindness.

The face that Akerman looked at all her life – her mother's
face – was taken from her only recently: Nelly died last year.
The daughter found herself suddenly alone. And just not any
daughter, but a Jew of the "second generation", with knowledge
of the horror her parent had suffered. What can it have been to
be the beloved and life-sustaining child of such a woman?

Our journey through her films has now been tragically
interrupted, just as it neared its end. Naïvely, we believed that her
film-making might continue indefinitely: we had just extended the
retrospective to allow for the screening of her latest – now last –
film *No Home Movie*, a study of Nelly's final years.

Chantal's voice, her face, her body, her life, her past, her
ancestral past – all these are, for those of us who have travelled
through her work, now imprinted on us forever.

(Kind permission to reprint: Catherine Shoard, *The Guardian*.)

Farewell: An homage to Chantal Akerman (1950 – 2015)

Frieze magazine, issue 176, January – February 2016.

As always, in the immediate aftermath of an artist's death, a sifting of the work is underway. Much has been written about the facts of Akerman's life; this supplements the revealing autobiographical details and allusions to be found in many of her films. However, a discussion of her lesser-known works may also be a good way of reflecting on her seemingly inexhaustible and marvellously varied body of work. Everything that Akerman produced deserves minute consideration, for she was a generous and prolific artist.

Taking Notice

D'Est: au bord de la fiction (*From the East: Bordering on Fiction*, 1993). Akerman said she wanted to make this film before it was 'too late'. But too late for what? Soviet communism was teetering and the old order was about to crumble. But so, too, was a cinema based on photochemical photography; documentary's moment was dawning. Akerman travelled behind the tattered Iron Curtain with a 16mm camera and returned with this startling series of observations and slow tracking shots examining the gaunt faces of the steadfast survivors of history. These are the ghosts of a narrative that cannot be told with words. Speech is, in any case, at a premium in a fractured world, where ideologies of all kinds subsume everything; perhaps it is simply better to listen to sentimental pop while preparing dried sausage for a lonely supper. What emerges is profound, and compassionate.

Chaplinesque

L'Homme à la valise (*The Man in a Suitcase*, 1983). An apartment in Paris: 'Chantal' arrives home after travelling abroad only to find a house guest has wildly outstayed his welcome.

The noise he makes drives Chantal mad, not least because she is creatively blocked and desperate for peace and quiet. Franz Kafka's unfinished short story, *The Burrow* (1931), springs to mind. The plot seems trite, but this droll comedy allows for the free play and clowning of the sort that had launched Akerman's career in *Saute ma ville* (1968). Onscreen, Chantal is delightfully energetic; her presence focused and committed, her rhythms angled and perfectly timed. Words are never needed; her physicality gives us more than enough.

Less is More

Un Jour Pina a demandé ... (One Day Pina Asked ..., 1983). Akerman knows what choreography is: the placing and moving of bodies in space and time. Pina Bausch was a German choreographer and dancer born in 1940; Akerman was a Jew, most of whose family was murdered by the Nazis. But both were great artists. Of all attempts to register on film something essential about dance and performance, this is arguably the greatest, not because of what is shown (so much is not) nor because of what is said (a brief conversation between the two is a damp squib), but because Akerman leads us into the heart of the matter by means of abrupt cuts between time and movement, and interviews whose point seems indeterminate. The effect is a crystalline representation of the emotion of the encounter – of clear speech without words. The familiar advice, to show not tell, is superbly obeyed.

Growing Pains

Portrait d'une jeune fille de la fin des années 60 à Bruxelles (Portrait of a Young Girl from the Late Sixties in Brussels, 1993). Commissioned for television, this film was shot on 16mm and focuses on a teenage schoolgirl falling in love with her lovely girlfriend: surely an episode from Akerman's own life. On one level, it might seem like a familiar form of scripted drama but, on the other, there is so much here that is unlike what you normally see on television: sustained takes, faces observed as they listen and react, the careful capture of a fleeting emotion, a moment of disappointed expectation that dissipates in real time. Akerman is careful enough to allow her camera to roll on past the point at which others might have lost interest, allowing our minds and feelings to fill the space left so carefully open for us. The final scene – at a dance when it becomes clear that this love will be unrequited – is one of the most heart-rending in all of cinema.

Musicality

Avec Sonia Wieder-Atherton (*With Sonia Wieder-Atherton*, 2002) and *Les Trois dernières sonates de Franz Schubert* (*Franz Schubert's Last Three Sonatas*, 1989). Akerman loved music. She would sometimes sing spontaneously – in fact, at one of our screenings, she took the microphone and sang Lionel Richie's 'Hello!' (1983). She loved all kinds of music – from Jewish liturgical music and popular songs to 1960s pop, French chansons and classical. In 1989, she made a film for French TV with the pianist Alfred Brendel. He plays and talks about Schubert, but what is remarkable is Akerman's illuminating insights into the nature of film and of her own artistic project. Hers is an art of selection, of framing, of moving closer – or not. It is a patient art. Later, her close relationship with the great cellist Sonia Wieder-Atherton gave rise to a series of films, made between 2002 and 2009, about music. They are showcases for Wieder-Atherton, of course, but are created as if the camera and the edit were another kind of instrument. In retrospect, Akerman's entire project feels essentially musical.

Mother

News from home (1977). Akerman's mother, Natalia or Nelly, is threaded through all of her films. Even when she's isn't there

herself, a character or situation references her. In News from
home, Akerman is 26 and living in New York and her mother
worries about her, as any mother would. But Akerman is
preoccupied by her mother, too, even if sometimes she would
rather not be. We hear Akerman reading her mother's letters;
her voice is in her daughter's head, therefore in our heads.
Akerman brings us close to the New York that her mother
cannot see and imagines to be dangerous, but Akerman shows
us the streets are safe; people go about their daily routine and
sometimes are curious enough to stare back at the camera.

Song
Nuit et Jour (*Night and Day*, 1991). All of Akerman's films are
songs. When we first met her in 2014, she sang Don McLean's
'American Pie' (1971) to us, as we walked along Marylebone
Road in London. We joined in:

A long, long time ago I can still remember how That music
used to make me smile And I knew if I had my chance That I
could make those people dance And maybe they'd be happy for
a while...

Akerman herself was like a character from a Jacques Demy
musical or, indeed, one of her own musicals. Not for nothing
was she named 'Chantal'; in French, 'chant' means 'song'.

New Wave
From the opening scenes of *J'ai faim, j'ai froid* (*I Am Hungry,
I Am Cold*, 1984), New Wave mannerisms are invoked with
a call-and-response between the film's two female protagonists.
Naughty girls run wild on a trip to Paris, picking up lovers,
singing for their supper, smoking, starving, not caring. Think
François Truffaut or early Jean-Luc Godard. Akerman was never
one to adopt someone else's style or idiom, nor to make direct
reference to other films, and yet here she seems to be enjoying
the break with her own tradition, breezily making her very own

New Wave cinema. She's part of a community of film-makers –
not, this time, the loner or the one who has to bear the burden
of being a prophetess of a new kind of cinema.

Nelly Dies

The 2014 screening we organised of *Toute une nuit* (*A Whole
Night*, 1982) had a shadow cast over it. Akerman's mother had
just died and we told the audience before showing the film. We
were all saddened, imagining Akerman's distress. Through the
many autobiographical aspects of her films, we felt we had come
to understand something of what her mother meant to her. She
was Chantal's anchor, the person she came back to, the person
she felt most at home with.

Gustav Mahler set Friedrich Rückert's poem *Oft denk'
ich, sie sind nur ausgegangen* (*Often, I Think They've
Gone for Just a Moment*, 1833-34) to music in his song
cycle *Kindertotenlieder* (*Songs on the Death of Children*,
1901 – 04). Akerman used this sad music in the film:

I think they've gone for just a moment. Soon will they be
reaching back homewards in safety. The day is fine. Oh, have no
fear: They merely go on a longer walk. Indeed, they have but
just gone out now, And will be here at home in a moment …
(Translation by David Paley)

Akerman had rhythm. Every sound and image in her films
clocks in and out at a perfect tempo: the clip-clop of shoes
on a pavement, a door abruptly shutting. A physical reaction
courses through our bodies – exactly as the film-maker would
want it. She's talking to us with her body (and, of course, always
with her head).

Jouissance

Un Divan à New York (*A Couch in New York*, 1996). Pure
pleasure: a romantic comedy to beat them all. We want it to
end happily and Akerman doesn't deny us that pleasure – all

the corners of the story come together beautifully. When the building, the rooms, the walls and the bars of the balcony that separate the lovers become irrelevant (they literally climb over the silly contrivances that have kept them apart) – arbitrary physical constraints are evaporated in a single leap of cinematic abandon that make us cry out with happiness. This is cinema as a series of random obstacles suddenly transformed before our eyes into a cinema of joy.

Postscript

Pure sadness. When we first planned Akerman's retrospective, *No Home Movie* (2015) didn't exist, except, perhaps, in her mind. It never occurred to us that when we watched it for the first time, not only would we be mourning the death of Akerman's mother, but mourning the death of the film-maker herself – which feels almost like the death of cinema. You can read into this film whatever you like. An image of a tree moving violently in the desert wind, its branches always springing back, is an image of survival, yet there are no survivors here. Akerman created an unsurpassed body of work with all the richness and depth of a life lived fully and intensely. She never put a foot wrong. Why don't more people know this?

(With thanks to Jennifer Higgie, editor of *Frieze* for kind permission to reprint.)

Retrospective data

	date	start	title	year	theatrical licence	film print
1	26.9.13	19.30	*Saute ma ville*	1968	Paradise Films (PF)	Cinematek (C)
			L'enfant aimé ou Je joue à être une femme mariée	1971	PF	C
			Hotel Monterey	1972	PF	C
2	28.11.13	19.00	*La Chambre*	1972	PF	C
			Le 15/8	1973	PF	C
			Je tu il elle	1974	PF	C
3	12.12.13	19.00	*Jeanne Dielman, 23 Quai du Commerce, 1080 Bruxelles*	1975	PF	C
4	23.1.14	19.00	*News from home (English version)*	1976	PF	C
			News from home (French version)	1976	PF	Le Bureau Films
5	13.2.14	19.30	*Les Rendez-vous d'Anna*	1978	PF	C
6	13.3.13	20.00	*Dis-moi (aka Aujourd'hui, dis moi)*	1980	INA	INA
			Autour de Jeanne Dielman	1976	Sami Frey/ Chantal Akerman	PF
7	10.4.14	20.00	*Toute une nuit*	1982	PF	Wallonie Bruxelles International
8	24.4.14	19.00	*Les Années 80*	1983	PF	C
9	22.5.14	19.00	*Un Jour Pina a demandé*	1983	INA	INA
			L'homme à la valise	1983	INA	INA
10	12.6.14	20.00	*J'ai faim, j'ai froid*	1984	ICAV	C
			Lettre de cinéaste	1984	INA	INA
			Portrait d'une paresseuse	1986	ZDF	ZDF
			Le Marteau	1984	Centre Georges Pompidou	Centre Georges Pompidou

	date	start	title	year	theatrical licence	film print
			Rue Mallet-Stevens	1984	VRT	VRT
11	17.7.14	19.00	*Golden Eighties*	1986	PF	RBFA
12	18.9.14	19.00	*Letters Home*	1986	Centre Audiovisual (CASB) Simone de Beauvoir	CASB
13	23.10.14	19.00	*Histoires d'Amérique*	1989	Mallia Films	Mallia Films
14	13.11.14	19.00	*Les Trois dernières sonates de Franz Schubert*	1989	INA	INA
			Trois strophes sur le nom de Sacher	1989	Mallia Films	Mallia Films
			Le Déménagement	1992	Les Poissons Volants	Poissons Volants
15	11.12.14	19.00	*Nuit et Jour*	1991	PF	C
16	22.1.15	19.00	*D'Est*	1993	CBA	CBA
17	12.2.15	19.00	*Écrire contre l'oubli*	1991	Béatrice Soulé	Béatrice Soulé
			Family Business	1984	John Ellis	John Ellis
			Portrait d'une jeune fille de la fin des années 60 à Bruxelles	1993	ARTE	ARTE
18	12.3.15	19.00	*Le Jour où*	1997	Waka Films	Waka
			Un Divan à New York	1996	PF	C
19	23.4.15	18.40	*Chantal Akerman par Chantal Akerman*	1996	INA	INA
			Sud	1999	Doc & Film International (D&F)	D&F
20	28.5.15	19.00	*La Captive*	2000	Chemah IS	C
21	18.6.15	19.00	*De l'autre côté*	2002	D&F	D&F
22	16.7.15	18.40	*Avec Sonia Wieder-Atherton*	2003	Mallia Films	Naïve
			A l'est avec Sonia Wider Atherton, pts 1&2	2009	Mallia Films	Naïve
23	17.9.15	19.00	*Demain on déménage*	2004	Le Bureau	Le Bureau
24	1.10.15	19.00	*Là-bas*	2006	D&F	D&F
25	22.10.15	19.00	*La Folie Almayer*	2011	D&F	D&F
26	30.10.15	19.30	*No Home Movie*	2015	D&F	D&F

title	duration	original	projection	subtitles	translator	introduction (if not JH & ADR)
Saute ma ville	13'	35mm	35mm	not required		Nina Danino
L'enfant aimé ou Je joue à être une femme mariée	35'	16mm	16mm	*A Nos Amours*	Maconochie/ Penny Averill	
Hotel Monterey	65'	16mm	16mm	not required		
La Chambre	11'	16mm	16mm	not required		
Le 15/8	42'	16mm	16mm	not required		
Je tu il elle	86'	16/ 35mm	35mm	burnt in		
Jeanne Dielman, 23 Quai du Commerce, 1080 Bruxelles	201'	35mm	35mm	burnt in		Laura Mulvey
News from home (English version)	85 '	16mm	DCP	English dialogue		Xiaolu Guo
News from home (French version)	85'	16mm	16mm	no		
Les Rendez-vous d'Anna	127 '	35mm	35mm	yes		Chris Petit
Dis-moi (aka *Aujourd'hui, dis moi*)	46'	16mm	Digibeta	*A Nos Amours* cued live		Sylvie Beaufils
Autour de Jeanne Dielman	70'	video	digital	burnt in		
Toute une nuit	89'	35mm	35mm	burnt in		Richard Kwietniowski
Les Années 80	82'	video /35mm	35mm	burnt in		Lucy Cash + CA Q&A
Un Jour Pina a demandé	57'	16mm	Digibeta	*A Nos Amours*	Maconochie (CM)	
L'homme à la valise	60'	16mm	Digibeta	*A Nos Amours*	CM	
J'ai faim, j'ai froid	12'	35mm	35mm	*A Nos Amours*, cued live	CM	
Lettre de cinéaste	9'	16mm	digital	*A Nos Amours*	CM	
Portrait d'une paresseuse	14'	16mm	digital	*A Nos Amours*		Adam Roberts/ Louise Lyon
Le Marteau	4'	video	digital	*A Nos Amours*		Jo Blair/ Charlotte Lopez
Rue Mallet-Stevens	7'	video	digital	*A Nos Amours*		Adam Roberts/ Louise Lyon
Golden Eighties	96'	35mm	35mm	live cueing	PF	Carol Morley

title	duration	original	projection	subtitles	translator	introduction (if not JH & ADR)
Letters Home	104'	video	BetaSP	live cueing	PF	Claire Atherton
Histoires d'Amérique	92'	16mm	BetaSP	English dialogue		Ruth Novaczek
Les Trois dernières sonates de Franz Schubert	46'	video	Digibeta	English dialogue		
Trois strophes sur le nom de Sacher	12'	Betacam SP	BetaSP	not required		
Le Déménagement	37'	Betacam SP	Beta SP	Yes		
Nuit et Jour	90'	35mm	35mm	*A Nos Amours*, cued live	CM	Olaf Möller
D'Est	107'	16mm	16mm	not required	Keifer Taylor	
Écrire contre l'oubli	4'	35mm	BetaSP	*A Nos Amours*, cued live	CM	John Ellis
Family Business	18'	16mm	Digital	burnt in		
Portrait d'une jeune fille de la fin des années 60 à Bruxelles	60 '	16mm	Digibeta	burnt in		
Le Jour oú	7'	35mm	35mm	*A Nos Amours*, cued live		Adam Roberts /Ian Monk
Un Divan à New York	105'	35mm	35mm	not required		
Chantal Akerman par Chantal Akerman	63'	DigiBeta	Digibeta	burnt in		Muriel Tinel-Temple
Sud	71 '	video	Digibeta	not required		
La Captive	118'	35mm	35mm	live cueing		
De l'autre côté	103 '	video /16mm	Digibeta	burnt in		
Avec Sonia Wieder-Atherton	51'	video	DVD	burnt in		David Thompson
A l'est avec Sonia Wider Atherton, pts 1&2	87'	video	DVD	burnt in		
Demain on déménage	110 '	35mm	35mm	burnt in		Nick James
Là-bas	79'	video	Digibeta	burnt in		
La Folie Almayer	127 '	35mm	DCP	burnt in		Gregor Muir/ Claire Atherton
No Home Movie	113'	video	DCP	burnt in		JH/AR/ Claire Atherton

Not included in the retrsopective

Tombée de nuit sur Shanghai (2007)
Commissioned to mark the 50th anniversary of the
Gulbenkian Foundation, and premiered in the 2007
Cannes _Quinzaine des Réalisateurs_. It formed a part of the
portmanteau project _O Estado do Mundo_ (_State of The World_),
with contributions also from Ayisha Abraham, Wang Bing,
Pedro Costa, Vicente Ferraz, and Apichatpong Weerasethakul.
Akerman subsequently decided to present _Tombée de nuit_
in galleries only, with the addition of a few objects. This was
included in our Ambika P3 exhibition.

Hanging Out Yonkers

(1973, mute unedited rushes, 27' surviving)
This would have been Akerman's first foray into documentary –
perhaps. It was a commission to film young people in a Yonkers
youth project. Babette Mangolte shot on 16mm. Famously, the
footage was lost, though half of it has now been found and
digitised by the Cinémathèque Royale in Brussels.

Babette Mangolte told us that: "About half of the footage was
not after all lost in the subway by Chantal, as we once thought.
And so, in March 2016 I took the subway to go to Yonkers and
see the footage that had been found by the Cinémathèque.
I was so moved looking at it with Jane Stein and her friend
Mira, who had organised the job for Chantal in the first place.
Chantal was paid a little bit and I worked pro bono and used
my own lights. I'm not sure but we shot mostly inside with
lights and so I think what I saw in 2015 on a DVD was what we

had shot on Kodachrome. It was a great experience for both of us." (email 28 October 2016)

This new material became available to screen only after the retrospective. It proved any case it has since then been impossible to arrange a screening in London.

Hôtel des acacias (1982)
Akerman supervised students of film at INSAS (Institut national supérieur des arts du spectacle et des techniques de diffusion), and this was the result. For this retrospective, not regarded as a work by Akerman.

Mid-retrospective symposium

THE HAND-OUT

A Nos Amours Chantal Akerman day

Sunday 12 October 2014, 12 noon – 5pm.
JW3, 341 Finchley Rd, London NW3 6ET.

Audience, scholars, artists, film-makers and curators gather to celebrate the work of Chantal Akerman at the mid-point of the *A Nos Amours* complete retrospective showing at the ICA Cinema

Speakers / artists

Chantal Akerman, Rebecca Aldridge, Amy Croft, Ella Harris, Pia Ilonka, Amber Jacobs, Eve Marguerite, Griselda Pollock, Sarah Pucill, Alison Rowley, Muriel Tinel-Temple and Isabel Taube.

This event is supported by Film Hub London, managed by Film London (partner in BFI Film Audience Network, sponsored by the National Lottery). With thanks to JW3 for partnership in this event, and to Kate Ross in particular.

About Chantal Akerman day

We are delighted that Chantal Akerman will be joining us for a day dedicated to her work to mark the mid-point of the *A Nos Amours* complete retrospective at ICA Cinema in London.

The retrospective has reached mid-point.

It has been a slow retrospective, taking its time over a 24-month span to showcase the work of a great and important film-maker.

This is therefore a good time to take stock and reflect.

The day brings together audience, artists, film-makers, scholars and Chantal Akerman herself for a day of presentations, screenings and discussion. We are very grateful to be kindly and generously hosted by the JW3 Centre.

Detail

Griselda Pollock is Professor in the School of Fine Art, History of Art and Cultural Studies at the University of Leeds, and will deliver a keynote address. Her paper is titled *The Primal Scene*.

Dr Alison Rowley is Reader in Cultural Theory at the University of Huddersfield. She will speak on mother and other relations in two films by Chantal Akerman, and will lead discussion with Chantal Akerman.

Dr Muriel Tinel-Temple is an associate lecturer at Birkbeck, and will speak about Akerman's 80s films commissioned for TV.

Akerman also exerts a profound influence over artists and film-makers – and we are delighted that Sarah Pucill will speak and present her film *Fall in Frame* (2103). Also presenting work are: Rebecca Aldridge, artist, showing images and performing a text; Ella Harris, currently working towards a PhD, joins with artist Eve Marguerite to present a paper: *On Geography in Akerman's Films*; Pia Ilonka, Berlin-based artist, shows *Little Short Film* (2014); Amber Jacobs, artist film-maker and scholar at Birkbeck, presents: *Curds and Whey* (2013); Amy Croft, artist film-maker, presents her film: *grey sky blue* (2012) and Isabel Taube has given us her text, *Akerman's Art*, included in this brochure, written while engaged with the Critical Writing course at the Royal College of Art.

And finally, we will be joined by Chantal Akerman herself who will be in conversation with Alison Rowley, and with all of us generally.

About the retrospective

Chantal Akerman is a film-maker whose time has come: her work is news that stays news. It is a cinema that reinvents and redefines what film is and should be.

Akerman's work is superficially wide-ranging – it includes documentary and narrative, film and video, 16mm and 35mm, cinema and gallery – and yet her work is characterised by an uncompromising and singular sense of purpose.

What Akerman shows us, by means structural and otherwise, is nothing less than the human condition, a series of astonishing meditations on loneliness and anxiety, alienation and discomfort. Akerman so quickly, from her earliest work, established a startling and provocative project that is among the very greatest in European film.

As J Hoberman has said: "Comparable in force and originality to Godard or Fassbinder, Chantal Akerman is arguably the most important European director of her generation".

I don't feel like I belong, and that's without real pain, without pride. Pride happens. No, I'm just disconnected, from practically everything. I have a few anchors, and sometimes I let them go or they let me go, and I drift. That's most of the time. Sometimes I hang on for a few days, minutes, seconds, then I let go again. I can hardly look. I can hardly hear. Semi-blind, semi-deaf, I float. Sometimes I sink. But not quite. Something, sometimes a detail, brings me back to the surface, and I start floating again…

(From Akerman's voiceover to *Là-bas* (*Down There*, 2006.)

Programme

12.00   Projection: *Entretien avec ma mère (Interview with my mother)* (2007 Brussels) Chantal Akerman interviews her mother, Natalia Akerman

12.30   Adam Roberts & Joanna Hogg: the Akerman retrospective: context for the day

12.45   Amber Jacobs: talk and screening of *Curds & Whey* (2013, 3')

13.05   Pia Ilonka: *Little Short Film* (3')
         Introduced by Eve Marguerite.

13.15   Rebecca Aldridge

13.30   Amy Croft: *grey sky blue* (2012, 20')
         Introduced by Eve Marguerite.

14.00   break

14.20   Eve Marguerite & Ella Harris: *On Geography
         in Akerman's films*

14.30   Sarah Pucill: **talk** and screening of
         Fall in Frame (2009, 18')

15.00   Griselda Pollock

15.20   Muriel Tinel-Temple

15.40   Alison Rowley

16.00   break

16.10   Chantal Akerman

17.30   ends

Akerman's Art

by Isabel Taube

(Written within constraints: use no full stops, write alphabetically.)

Jeanne Dielman 23 Quai du Commerce, 1080 Bruxelles is a
film by Chantal Akerman and portrays a woman's austere
daily regime, where each task is anointed with an over-
attentiveness, both brutal and banal, as she buys bread and
searches for buttons in Brussels, boredom, biting into the
block of flats where she boils potatoes, busies herself before
clients and then greets them into her contained, cut-off
existence, the kitchen where she chops, cleans, contemplates,
collapses into chairs, is cornered by a sense of crisis, how to
dissolve time? Jeanne Dielman played by Delphine Seyrig is a
diligently dressed darting mother and widow, whose attempts
to divide each day are derailed in a sudden explosive
episode, enacted after a morning of errands – an encounter
between five and five-thirty – time forced, time fixed into
slots, time followed fretfully (the green tiles, the gas heater,
the gas hob burning in an empty kitchen) grinding down
each day she is haunted by an absence; hurriedly walking
through the dark hallway in and out of rooms she paces in
isolation, imposes order; Jeanne's clenched jaw, her joyless
existence, joining the world briefly, then journeying back to
the kitchen where she wipes knives, kneads meat, knocks
over cutlery, keeping all beneath a lid – she first takes the
scarves of the men as they enter – never explicitly lying to
her son, though little by little, ladling soup, after which she
leafs through the newspaper, tries to maintain herself, at
the premiere in Cannes Marguerite Duras stood up in the
middle, "this woman is mad," the next day Akerman's name
made: a new way of narrating and negotiating obsessive
compulsive disorder onscreen, the pressures of perfectionism
(for example, the coffee scene) performed carefully by

Seyrig, practical piecing and unpiecing, Akerman saw
Godard's *Pierrot le fou* as a teenager (a quote: "it's through
the making that I find my way"[1]) and so she returned to her
childhood, the quilt that Jeanne spreads out each morning,
the rituals and rhythms of her aunts and mother, recognising
in them a restlessness, a need to resist despair through
routine, reflected in the film's stasis, its long stretches of time
(scenes with no soundtrack, the situation slowly traversing)
two pieces of sugar, the china tureen, tiny details, two
hundred minutes, Chantal Akerman was twenty-four when
she shot *Jeanne Dielman* and had been living in New York
where she was witness to the underground film movement
(the narrative, however, returns to her upbringing in Belgium
and the undervalued domestic work of her mother), yet
Jeanne is not a vessel: for instance the way she prepares the
veal, the way the veal becomes the most important part of
the film, the veal is late and the value placed upon the veal,
that it must be ready on time, is not about virtue but vigilance
against oneself, she is not vitriolic when visited by the woman
upstairs (performed by Akerman) whom we never see but
who asks Jeanne what she should cook for dinner, instead she
veers away from her; her wearisome expression working itself
into the wallpaper, the yellow light, the yolk-coloured blouse
she wears, the pale yellow xanthine tiles, nothing is zoomed
in on, the camera waits, as we wait, there is distance, yet the
audience is intimate with this woman, we cannot zoom in,
only notice; the film, released in 1975, is seen as the zenith
of Akerman's career, after watching it, after having zoned
in for three and half hours on the interior of a woman's life
and all along the anticipation of the final scene, the anxious
approach and the aftermath, acted out so acutely by Seyrig;
the tiles and the hallway, the bed-spread, the click of the light

1 'Chantal Akerman in conversation with Ricky D'Ambrose', Partisan Films, Vimeo, recorded
November 2013.

switch as she leaves one room, enters another, before she sits at the table in the dark, exhausted, and cars pass by, their lights beaming against her face, it is as if one is caught, like Jeanne, within the moment of catastrophe.

(With thanks to Isabel Taube for permission to reproduce her text.)

Acknowledgments and thanks

ALPHABETICALLY

Thank you for permission to reprint texts: Sylviane Akerman, Fondation Akerman, Melissa Anderson (4Columns), Claire Atherton, Steven Ball, Raymond Bellour, Tiffany Boodram (Condé Nast), Richard Brody, Jean Claudel (Editions Amplitude), Bruno Dequen (Revue 24 images), Pierre-Antoine Devic (Naïve Classique), Clément Dirié (JRP Ringier Kunstverlag), Alan Fell, Gwendolyn Audrey Foster, Matthew Frost (Manchester University Press), Diane Grosse (Duke University Press), Rodney Grunes, Daryoush Haj-Najafi (*ICA Bulletin*), Tim Hayes (Warner Chappell), Jennifer Higgie (Frieze), Eva-Lynn Jagoe, Marcel Jean, Michael Koresky, Cybelle McFadden, David Paley, Marion Schmid, Catherine Shoard (Guardian Newspapers), Matthew Stevens (Flicks Books), Anna Thorngate (Criterion), Andrew Tracy (Cinema Scope), Karin Tucker (University of California Press), Ginette Vincendeau, Silvia Voser (Waka Films), Sonia Wieder-Atherton, Patricia Zline (Fairleigh Dickinson University Press).

Presenters: Claire Atherton, Lucy Cash, Nina Danino, John Ellis, Xiaolu Guo, Joanna Hogg, Nick James, Richard Kwietniowski, Olaf Möller, Carol Morley, Gregor Muir, Laura Mulvey, Ruth Novaczek, Chris Petit, Adam Roberts, Keifer Taylor, David Thompson, and Muriel Tinel-Temple.

Volunteers: Jon Crosland-Mills, Laura Crosland-Mills, Chahine Fellahi, Jessica Fletcher, Rosie Goddard, Kim Goldsmith, Ella Harris, Eve Marguerite, Ioana Salagean and Keifer Taylor.

Translations/help with translations: Penny Averill, Sylvie Beaufils, Jo Blair, Matteo Fargion, Danielle Gilbert, Charlotte Lopez, Louise Lyon, Charlotte Maconochie, Ann Malkin, David Paley, Adam Roberts, Rabbi Jeremy Rosen, Keith Seward, Magdalena Wójcik.

The book: Thanks to Lora Findlay for her beautiful book design, and her enthusiastic engagement with the ethos of the project. Thanks also to Matt Rance the Proof Professor for his careful correction of our text, not easy given the multilingual format. Thanks are due finally to our printers TJ International.

Thanks due to people and organisations:
Aurore Auguste, Le Bureau Films
Jo Blair, Picturehouse
Clémentine De Blieck, Royal Belgian Film Archive
Emilie Bourgin, Les Poissons Volants
James Burbidge, Regent Street Cinema
Jean-Pierre Caillet, Les Poissons Volants
Nina Chanay, Zeugma Films
Laura Cohen, Le Centre audiovisuel Simone de Beauvoir
Pauline Colin, Le Bureau
Philip Concannon
Aurore Crétel, Wallonie-Bruxelles International (WBI)
Brigitte Dieu, INA
Joële van Effenterre, Mallia Films
Bertrand van Effenterre, Mallia Films
Catherine Elwes
Denys Fleutot, ICAV
Lore Gablier, Paradise Films/Chemiah IS
Bernadette Gazzola-Dirrix, INA
Sophie Guyon, AMIP
Rym Hachimi, Le Bureau
Clare Harwood, BFI

Hannah Horner, Doc & Film International
May Adadol Ingawanij, University of Westminster
Gerhard Kassner
Christoph Jacobs, ZDF
Linda De Leeuw, VRT
Shira MacLeod, Regent Street Cinema
Babette Mangolte
Godfrey Marriott
Michael Mazière, Ambika P3
Charles MacDonald
Flora Menzies, Film London
Saskia Nilly, Les Poissons Volants
Delphine Pertus, ARTE
Judith Revault d'Allonnes, Centre Georges Pompidou
Lucy Reynolds at University of Westminster
Paul Ridd, Picturehouse
Béatrice Soulé
Rosie Thomas, University of Westminster
Thierry Vandersanden, Ministère de la communauté française
Jean-Jacques Varret, Les Films du paradoxe
Eléonore Venti, Wallonie-Bruxelles International (WBI)
Karine de Villiers, Le CBA

At the ICA: Maya Caspari, Sophie Coke-Steel, Naomi Crowther, Lucia Genziani, Aran Gillies, Tim Hale, Emily Hawden, Roger Holland, James King, Jonathan Lowe, Kathryn Lloyd, Victor Makourin, Nico Marzano, Ben Moon, Gregor Muir, Nick Olorenshaw, David Powell, Annie Rudnick, Nick Santos-Pedro. The ICA front-of-house team of whose names we did not take proper note, but who were always superb.

Mid-Symposium Retrospective (speaking or showing work): Rebecca Aldridge, Amy Croft, Kate Greenspon, JW3, Ella Harris, Pia Ilonka, Amber Jacobs, Eve Marguerite, Professor Griselda

Pollock, Sarah Pucill, Dr Alison Rowley, Isabel Taube, Dr Muriel Tinel-Temple.

Thanks are very much due also for the constant love and support of Louise Lyon.

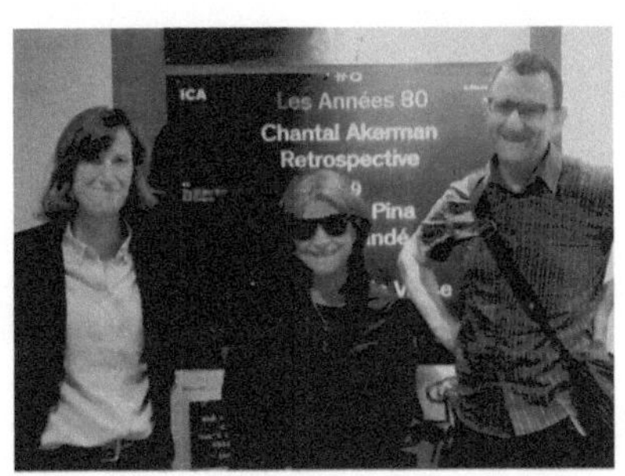

To Chantal Akerman
we offer thanks and gratitude for
generous help and support in mounting
this retrospective, for her friendship,
and above all for the gift
to us all of her work.